EVERY monday→ MATTERS

Published in Nashville, Tennessee, by Thomas Nelson, Inc.

Project Editor: Lisa Stilwell
Designed by Leonardo Canneto /materialdesign.com
Photography by Jonathan W. Brown / jonathanbrownphotography.com

ISBN-10: 1-4041-0512-3
ISBN-13: 978-1-4041-0512-6

Printed and bound in the United States

www.thomasnelson.com

EVERY →
monday
MATTERS

52 ways to make a difference

Matthew Emerzian and Kelly Bozza

Design by Leonardo Canneto
Photography by Jonathan W. Brown

THOMAS NELSON
Since 1798

NASHVILLE DALLAS MEXICO CITY RIO DE JANEIRO BEIJING

Dedication

Momma Choda and Pops,
I came from your heart
so that I may come from mine.
Thank you for the life and the love.
  Matthew

Mom and Dad,
For endowing me with acts of love
that enlighten my life and
for teaching me how to lighten another's.
  Kelly

To all of you who truly make a difference
each and every day...
You matter.

INTRODUCTION
have you made today matter?

Millions of people each year want to
know how to make a difference—in their lives and the lives of others.
Millions of people each year want to
focus on what's important—what really matters.

If you're like most people,
you want to contribute,
make a difference, and have a positive impact,
but, m a y b e
you don't know what to do,
where to go,
when the "right" time is, or
how to get others involved.

Every Monday Matters
is here to help.

This "involvement" guide book provides a straightforward, uncomplicated,
and down-to-earth process for getting YOU involved
and to help you get OTHERS involved.

WHY MONDAY?

Before now, Monday was the least favorite day of the week. Monday was the day that ended your weekend; the day you HAD to go back to work; and the day you started a diet or decided to not smoke another cigarette. . .again.

WHY MONDAY? 52

Our goal is to change the "image" of Mondays by making them mean something **amazing**, something **incredible**, something **unbelievable**. From this day forward, we'll show you how to make your Mondays matter!

52 mondays
52 activities
52 ways to make a difference

As you flip
through these
pages, you will see that every
Monday has an activity that makes
it easy for you to move from just thinking
or talking about being of service to actually taking action.
Being of service comes in many shapes and sizes. Some weeks'
activities are simpler than others, but they all pack a big punch.
For example, on **Monday #8**, the **Every Monday Matters** activity is to
help the hungry by simply donating some of your time or food.
On **Monday #21**, the **Every Monday Matters** activity is to **learn CPR**
so you are equipped to save someone's life in the case of an emergency.
As you participate in each week's activities, you'll see that **Every Monday Matters**
is incredibly simple, yet significant, and has little to do
with how much time it takes or **the size of the action**.

ordinary people
doing extraordinary good

It amazes us how a simple conversation can turn into a book.
We were talking about why we do the things we do—donate blood, spend time with foster children, change our lightbulbs to conserve energy, and bring flowers to an elderly neighbor.

While we know how to fill a need, make someone smile, use less energy, and be neighborly, we're not experts in medicine, psychology, the environment, or our community. We're not even experts in writing books. But what we are experts in is **making a difference** in a small **but significant way.** In other words, **WE'RE JUST LIKE YOU.**

Knowing **how busy life can be**, we knew that we had to offer compelling reasons why you should want to do each Monday's activity. We also recognize **how precious time is**, so we created this book to be easy to read and, more importantly, easy to do. **We are confident you will see what we mean.**

First, you will see that each Monday is written to be informative and enlightening, offering United States–based facts, unless otherwise noted, to give you a clear picture of why there is a need. The statistics are mind-boggling and, oftentimes, unsettling. **Second**, we give you a specific plan for exactly what you can do and where you can go to make a difference. It's an appointment you won't want to miss. **Third**, we illustrate the benefit of your actions and the collective actions of many. Three hundred million empowered individuals is a lot of extraordinary good.

ITCHANGESYOU

From firsthand experience, we can say that **our lives have changed**. The day we cooked and served dinner to families living in transitional living situations, we had many feelings throughout the experience—concern that anyone could be one paycheck away from homelessness; gratitude for family, friends, co-workers, and spiritual relationships; **excitement about doing something so meaningful;** and sadness that in our own community we have people who don't know how they are going to get their next meal.

Although we made an **impact on people's lives**, they made an unforgettable impression on our soul.

We've found that...

It's fulfilling to be both valuable to someone and **valued**.

When you gravitate toward what brings you happiness, **happiness gravitates toward you**.

It is more rewarding to **lift someone up** than to let someone down.

You can **give away** yet still feel filled up.

Working for **free can be more** significant than working for money.

To **consume less** doesn't mean that we live without.

Satisfying someone else's needs can be a great source of **self-satisfaction**.

When we befriend our neighbor, **we benefit the world**.

Making the world a better place is a **LABOR OF LOVE**.

becommitted

it's not EVERY monday or NO mondays

We want you to make every Monday matter, but we are also realistic. We want you to make a commitment to yourself. We promise that you will get so much out of the Mondays that you won't want to skip one, and if you do, you won't wait months before you participate again.

We want you to make **Every Monday Matter**, but we are also realistic.
So make a commitment to yourself.
We promise that you will get so much out of Mondays that you won't want to skip one.
And, if you do, **you won't wait months before you participate again.**

We recommend that you do each Monday's activity alongside **friends and family**. That way you can share experiences and hold each other accountable. You'll also have more fun and find it **harder to quit.**

Your **Mondays** will empower you and stretch you.
They will provide a sense of **accomplishment**,
make you more **compassionate**,
reward you in ways you never expected,
cause you to be annoyed that more people aren't there to **help**...

...and infect you with an enthusiasm that is so contagious **that you will get more people involved each and every week.**

GET**STARTED**

It starts with **YOU**
who turns to your friend, neighbor, co-worker, significant other,
and says, "We need to do this!"

This is about people taking
personal responsibility to make a difference.
To matter—one day, one action at a time.

While the ideas in this book can be put into action
one person at a time,
our vision extends far beyond the individual.
It is a simple game of numbers...
**a community of friends,
a chamber of commerce,
a neighborhood,
a church,
a club,
employees at a company...**
and grows across the nation.
Imagine a day when no one honks their horn.
Imagine a day when there are 300 million fewer pieces of litter
on the streets because everyone picked up just one piece of trash.
**Imagine a day when...
Imagine.**

Reading **about why you're needed doesn't make a difference.**
Thinking **about doing something doesn't make a difference.**
Getting started DOES make a difference.

everymondaymatters.com

You have the power to make a difference.
WE JUST WANT TO HELP.
USE THE TOOLS...

EveryMondayMatters.com is here to support **you.** For every Monday activity described in this book, you will find creative ideas, answers to FAQs, lists of organizations to support in your desired area of interest, zip code tools to help you find locations near you, and much more.

At EveryMondayMatters.com we want to make **making a difference** as **easy as possible,** so visit us each and every week.

Please share with us—and with others—how your Mondays have touched your heart and made a difference in your life as **you were making a difference in someone else's.**

We encourage you to post your photos, videos, experiences, and ideas with us.

We want to hear about it.
ENJOY THE EXPERIENCE.

YouMatterToday

Here is your list of 52 ways to make a difference.
You are very important to this movement.
Don't take your role lightly.

Start this Monday. **Don't wait until next Monday.**
One check mark a week. **It's simple, so get started.**

Name: _____

Date: _____

- [ ] 1 What Matters Most
- [ ] 2 Turn Off Your TV
- [ ] 3 Have AMBER Alerts Sent to You
- [ ] 4 Prepare for an Emergency
- [ ] 5 Eat Healthy
- [ ] 6 Get Rid of Junk Mail
- [ ] 7 Write a Letter to a U.S. Military Hero
- [ ] 8 Help the Hungry
- [ ] 9 Protect Yourself with Internet Safety
- [ ] 10 Change Your Lightbulbs
- [ ] 11 Register to Vote
- [ ] 12 Party with a Purpose
- [ ] 13 Donate Books
- [ ] 14 Create, Support, Appreciate Art
- [ ] 15 Rideshare
- [ ] 16 Support Neighborhood Watch
- [ ] 17 Register to Donate Your Organs
- [ ] 18 Show Your Smile
- [ ] 19 Adopt a Pet
- [ ] 20 Don't Flick Your Cigarette Butt
- [ ] 21 Learn CPR
- [ ] 22 Thank a Firefighter
- [ ] 23 Get Tested
- [ ] 24 Don't Honk
- [ ] 25 Plant a Tree
- [ ] 26 Support a Global Cause
- [ ] 27 Protect Yourself from Identity Theft
- [ ] 28 No Fast Food
- [ ] 29 Write a Note of Gratitude
- [ ] 30 Create a Back-to-School Backpack
- [ ] 31 Treat the Homeless with Dignity
- [ ] 32 Don't Drive over the Speed Limit
- [ ] 33 Read a Book
- [ ] 34 Pick Up Litter
- [ ] 35 Go Exercise
- [ ] 36 Be Neighborly
- [ ] 37 Mentor a Child
- [ ] 38 Donate Blood
- [ ] 39 Have Fun with an Elderly Person
- [ ] 40 Thank a Local Law Enforcement Officer
- [ ] 41 Choose Canvas Bags
- [ ] 42 Give a Hug
- [ ] 43 Listen, Play, Appreciate Music
- [ ] 44 Use Online Bill Pay
- [ ] 45 Get Involved with Foster Kids
- [ ] 46 Donate Clothes
- [ ] 47 Meditate or Pray
- [ ] 48 Respect the Disabled
- [ ] 49 Reduce, Reuse, Recycle
- [ ] 50 Thank a Teacher
- [ ] 51 No Nicotine
- [ ] 52 Your Day

**EVERYONE
has the
POWER OF GREATNESS.
Not for fame,
but greatness.**

Because greatness is determined by SERVICE.

- Dr. Martin Luther King, Jr.

WHAT MATTERS MOST!

- FAMILY
- FRIENDS
- FAITH
- HEALTH
- LOVE
- CAREER
- HAPPINESS
- PETS

The
list
you've
never
made.

make today matter...

whatmattersmost

FACTS

The average person spends:
- **100 hours** a year commuting to work compared to 80 hours of vacation time.
- **91 hours** a week at work for dual-career couples with kids.
- **1.8 hours** a day doing household activities.
- **2.6 hours** a day watching television.
- **8.6 hours** a day sleeping.

Time is a non-renewable resource.
Once it's used up,
you can't get it back.

TAKE ACTION TODAY

1. **Stop and think**…then make a list of what matters most to you.
2. **Create a list** of how you currently spend your time each week.
3. **Organize** your list of weekly activities and identify activities that are required and those that are optional and waste time.
4. Take steps to **rearrange** your schedule or reduce the optional activities so that you can spend time doing **what matters most.**
5. **Don't waste time.**

YOU MATTER

What really matters most to you?

Your relationships with family, friends, and children? Helping others? Passions? Faith? Security? Health? At the end of each year, don't you want to look back and see that you made a difference? That you matter? Today is the start of a new year.

Start it off by making a difference in you, in your life, and in the lives of those you love.

This is your opportunity.

Time spent on what matters most is never a waste of time.

turn Off your tv

FACTS

- 99% of all homes **have at least one TV**—45% have three or more.
- 56% of all 8- to 16-year-olds have a **TV in their bedroom.**
- A person watches TV an **average of 40 days per year.**
- Children spend **1,023 hours a year watching TV** compared to **900 hours in school.**
- **200,000 violent acts**, including **16,000 murders**, will be seen on TV by children before their 18th birthday.
- Roughly 70% of all TV shows include sexual content, with an average of **five sexual scenes per hour.**
- On average, **38.5 minutes per week of meaningful conversation** happens between a parent and their child.

TAKE ACTION TODAY

1. **Turn off your TV today.**
2. Designate certain TV-free times throughout the week to reduce viewing hours.
3. **Remove TVs from bedrooms, kitchen, etc.**
4. **Make a list of activities** to do besides watching TV—activities like reading, biking, swimming, walking, gardening, or socializing with friends. **Then start doing them.**
5. **Avoid using TV as a reward—this only increases its power.**
6. Be more selective about programming and choose history, travel, cooking, home repair/design, and other educational themes.

YOU MATTER

70% of people say that no matter how hard they try, they never seem to have enough time to do everything they need to do. Are you part of that 70%? If you give up TV for just one day a week, you can exercise for the recommended weekly amount necessary for healthy living, read over 20 books a year, or spend more time with your loved ones. **instead of watching reruns of *FRIENDS* go make some.**

what if it was YOUR CHILD?

Have AMBER Alerts sent to you

FACTS

AMBER stands for
"America's Missing: Broadcast Emergency Response"
and was created as a legacy to 9-year-old Amber Hagerman,
who was kidnapped while riding her bicycle in Arlington, Texas,
then brutally murdered.

- **76%** of abducted children who are murdered are dead within
  3 hours of the abduction and 88.5% are dead within 24 hours.
- **336 children have been reunited with their**
  families because of AMBER Alerts.
- **70%** of people with cell phones are eligible to receive Wireless
  AMBER Alerts as text messages.
- **100%** of computers can have the **AMBER Alert ticker**
  downloaded onto them.
- **AMBER Alerts** are **active in ALL 50 states.**

TAKE ACTION TODAY

1. Pay attention to **AMBER Alert**
signs on the freeway or on TV.
2. Sign up to receive **AMBER Alert**
text messaging on your cell phone.
3. Download the **AMBER Alert**
ticker onto your computer.
4. If you see or receive an
AMBER Alert signal,
don't take it lightly.
The perpetrator might
be closer than you
think.

YOU MATTER

Protecting children from abduction and locating those who have been abducted is the twofold purpose of
AMBER Alerts. They increase the number of people who can **help locate an abducted child** or
deter predators, and they have caused perpetrators to release the abducted child after hearing or seeing
the AMBER Alert. Remember, those first three hours are everything to that child and his or her family.
Your eyes and action could mean the difference between a life lost and a life saved.

Let's help to reunite them.

Predict the unpredictable.

PREDICT THE UNPREDICTABLE.

make today matter...

Prepare For An EMERGENCY

FACTS

-800 tornadoes are reported annually.
-The average path of a twister is 660 feet wide and up to 50 miles long.
-39 states are considered at risk of an earthquake.
-46% of disaster deaths occur due to floods.
-Because of contamination, clean water is harder to find than food after a flood.
-A tropical storm becomes a hurricane when the speed of its winds reaches 74 mph.
-September 11, 2001, will always be a reminder of the reality of terrorist attacks and the damage they can cause.

TAKE ACTION TODAY

1. Develop a **family communication plan** by selecting a person outside your local area for everyone to call in case of an emergency.
2. Ensure every member of your family knows the phone number and has coins or a prepaid phone card for calling the emergency contact. Cell phones often get jammed due to high call volume during disasters.
3. Designate a primary and secondary meeting location.
4. Create an emergency supply kit with a 3-day supply of basic items such as: fresh water, food, first aid, towelettes, garbage bags, a flashlight with extra batteries, local maps, a whistle, dust masks, tools, a can opener, and cash. Check and rotate supplies every 6 months.

YOU MATTER

Disasters are never planned, but they will happen. ***They are inevitable.***
Being prepared is the only thing **you can do.**
Having proper supplies and a well-thought-out plan **can make all the difference in your survival.**
Readiness will also reduce fear, anxiety, and potential losses.

PREPARE TODAY...FOR ANY KIND OF TOMORROW.

Can you really afford not to?

eat**HEALTHY**

French fries are the most widely eaten vegetable.

FACTS

- Annual cost for chronic conditions and diseases is big money:
  - **$117 billion for obesity**
  - **$66 billion for high blood pressure**
  - **$432 billion for heart disease and strokes**
  - **$50 billion for weight-loss aids**, diet foods, supplements, and weight-loss medications, **yet obesity is still increasing.**
- *79% likelihood exists that an overweight child will become an overweight adult.*
- 75% of adults don't eat the recommended daily 5 or more servings of fruits and vegetables.
- Snack consumption by children has **increased 300%** from 20 years ago.
- **400,000 people die annually from poor eating habits and laziness.**

TAKE ACTION TODAY

1. If you suffer from or have a family history of any of the aforementioned chronic conditions or diseases, **consult your family physician** for dietary counseling.

2. Although every individual is unique in his or her dietary needs, **here are some ideas to help**:
  - Eat fewer foods with refined grains and sugars; reduce your intake of fatty foods; and eat smaller portions.
  - Eat more dark green vegetables, legumes, fruits, whole grains, low-fat milk products, and lean meats.
  - **Eat slowly so that you will feel full before you've overeaten.**
  - **Don't reward yourself or children with food.**
  - **Develop a routine and eat at similar times each day.**
  - **Drink plenty of water.**
  - **Limit snacking.**

3. Eat to live; don't live to eat.

YOU MATTER

You deserve to be in good health. *For most, diabetes, hypertension, and other obesity-related chronic diseases are preventable by simply eating healthily and exercising. You will feel better than ever both mentally and physically—the only way to really live. If you don't want to do it for yourself or your wallet,* **do it for those who love you.**

Just start ... one day at a time.

how many trees
fit in your
mailbox?

get rid of junk mail

FACTS

- **Junk-mail deliveries surpass the number of U.S. Postal Service 1st-class mail.**
- Even though 44% of all junk mail is discarded without being opened, people will still spend 8 months of their lives opening junk mail.
- **Only 2% of junk mail gets a response.**
- 100 million trees are needed to produce the annual supply of bulk mail—that's the equivalent of deforesting the entire Rocky Mountain National Park every four months.
- Over $350 million taxpayer dollars are spent annually to dispose of junk mail that does not get recycled.
- **5.6 million tons of catalogs and other direct-mail advertisements end up in landfills annually.**
- The average person receives only 1.5 personal letters each week compared to 10.8 pieces of junk mail.
- **Paper will take up 48% of our landfills by 2010.**

TAKE ACTION TODAY

1. Write "Please do not rent or sell my name" next to your name whenever you enter a contest, make a purchase or donation, join a buyer's club, order a product by mail, subscribe to a magazine, or return a warranty card.
2. Call the customer service number of the company or organization that is sending you unwanted mail and ask to be removed from their list.
3. Remove your name from several national mailing lists through the Direct Marketing Association's Mail Preference Service. You can register online or by mail.
4. Contact major consumer credit bureaus to have your name removed from mailing lists used for credit offers.

YOU MATTER

500 pieces of junk mail per person per year...what a waste.
By decreasing your junk mail, **you'll save trees, save waste, decrease pollution, save time,** *and save the mail carrier's back because he or she won't have to deliver* **mail that you don't read anyway.**

WRITE A LETTER
TO A U.S. MILITARY HERO

monday
07

FACTS

- There are approximately **2.1 million active and reserve men and women** in the U.S. military.
- Hundreds of thousands of troops are deployed indefinitely in remote parts of the world, including the Middle East, Afghanistan, Africa, the Korean Peninsula, and on ships throughout international waters.
- Active military members are deployed for long periods of time, and they love receiving good wishes and words of appreciation and support, even from total strangers.
- **The most requested item by military men and women is a letter.**

TAKE ACTION TODAY

1. Select a soldier you know or one who is related to someone you know.
2. If you don't know a soldier, ask a friend, fellow student, co-worker, pastor, or military chaplain to help you make a connection. Make sure they provide proper mailing instructions.
3. Grab some paper, an envelope, and a pen.
4. Write a letter from your heart **that expresses your gratitude, shows your support, and provides encouragement.** Share a little bit about yourself and ask questions. Avoid such topics as death, killing, and politics.
5. Include your e-mail or mailing address in case the recipient wants to write back.
6. Send the letter.

YOU MATTER

Our military protects our nation's freedom, and, regardless of your political affiliation and **whether or not you believe in war,** these brave men and women need to know that **we appreciate their sacrifices and service.** With a simple card or letter, you can brighten the day of a soldier who is overseas ensuring your freedom.

YOUR LETTER MIGHT BE THE ONLY THING
THAT MAKES A SOLDIER SMILE THAT DAY.

Ever been hungry ...for a week?

help the Hungry

FACTS

- **The 2nd largest expense for families is food.**
- 35.1 million Americans have limited access to enough food due to a lack of money and other resources.
  12.4 million of those are children.
- 30% of families are forced to choose between buying food and paying for medical care or medicine.
- Many soup kitchens serve up to 1,000 meals a week. They need volunteers year-round, especially during holidays.
- **1 in 4 people in a soup kitchen line is a child.**

96 billion pounds of food are wasted each year.

TAKE ACTION TODAY

1. Locate organizations near you that **support** the hungry. Find out what those organizations need and help provide it.
2. Donate your time and **volunteer** at a food pantry/distribution center, a local soup kitchen, or a homeless shelter.
3. Go through your pantry and gather up canned and dried foods to **donate**.
4. **Create** or support a local canned food drive.
5. **Purchase and hand out** fast-food gift cards to homeless people. Buy extra cards to have on hand for **spontaneous giving**.

YOU MATTER

Most people don't have to decide between buying food, paying rent, and purchasing medicine or medical care. But, the sad truth is, millions do. Whether you personally **donate time**, money, canned foods, or restaurant gift cards, **you can be part of the solution**. And, as you strive to end hunger, you will gain a new appreciation for the food you have on your table at home... **it truly is a blessing.**

ARE YOU
PROTECTED?

Protect Yourself with Internet Safety

FACTS

- **61.8% of all households have a computer.**
- 54.7% of those households have Internet access.
- 9% of identity theft information is obtained online.
- **1 million Internet users believe they have received a phishing e-mail.**

  (Phishing is the act of sending an e-mail to a user falsely, claiming to be an established legitimate enterprise in an effort to **steal the user's personal information.**)

- 3.8 days is the average life span of a phishing Web site.
- **2 million adult Internet users experience Internet identity fraud annually—5,479 a day.**

TAKE ACTION TODAY

1. Create a password that has a combination of upper- and lowercase letters, numbers, and symbols for unlocking your computer and for accessing Web sites. Use a different password for each site.

2. Never use an automatic log-in feature that saves your username and password.

3. Always log off the Internet or your computer when you're finished.

4. Avoid storing financial information on your computer.

5. Use anti-virus software and a firewall.

6. Do not open e-mails sent to you by strangers.

7. Forward spam that is phishing for information to spam@uce.gov and to the company, bank, or organization impersonated in the phishing e-mail.

YOU MATTER

The emotional impact of Internet identity fraud has been found to **parallel that of victims of violent crime.** Remain cyber-safe by protecting your computer as if it were your wallet. **Practice safe surfing.** You'll be glad you did.

Finally...A bright idea.

Change Your Lightbulbs

FACTS

- **75% less energy is used with an ENERGY STAR—labeled compact fluorescent lightbulb (CFL) compared to a standard incandescent bulb (regular lightbulb).**
- ENERGY STAR was introduced by the EPA as a voluntary labeling program designed to help businesses and individuals choose energy-efficient products wisely and better protect the environment.
- **CFLs last up to 10 times longer and save $30 over the life of the bulb.**
- CFLs are safer because they produce less than 100°F of heat compared to halogen bulbs at 1000°F.
- **Replacing 1 bulb prevents the release of 300 pounds of carbon dioxide in just 1 year.**
- Switching just 1 bulb in every household would reduce carbon dioxide by 90 billion pounds a year.
- **If every home replaces 5 frequently used lightbulbs with CFLs, close to $8 billion a year in energy costs could be saved.**

TAKE ACTION TODAY

1. Buy a package of CFL bulbs today.

2. Refer to the lumen or light output on the product packaging as your guide to determine correct wattage.

3. Replace at least 1 regular lightbulb with a CFL bulb. The more bulbs you change, the better it is for the environment and your wallet.

4. Place qualified CFLs in the fixtures you use most frequently.

5. Use qualified CFLs in the fixtures that are hard to reach such as ceiling fans, other ceiling fixtures, and enclosed outdoor fixtures.

6. Call your local waste management company to ask for proper disposal methods: CFL bulbs should not be thrown away in your home or office garbage can. Many major retailers also offer take-back programs.

YOU MATTER

The amount of pollution equivalent to the emissions of two million cars can be removed from the atmosphere if every household in America replaces one lightbulb with an ENERGY STAR—qualified CFL bulb.

One bulb. Will you do it? How about five?

If you register...you'll vote.

Register to Vote

FACTS

- Voter registration has a dramatic impact on voter turnout.
- In the 2004 presidential election:
  - **88.5% of registered voters voted**—only 63.8% of total voting-eligible population.
  - **88% of registered men voted**—only 62.1% of all men.
  - **89% of registered women voted**—only 65.4% of all women.
  - **81.2% of registered 18- to 24-year-olds voted**—only 46.7% of all 18- to 24-year-olds.
  - **92.1% of registered 65- to 74-year-olds voted**—only 73.3% of all 65- to 74-year-olds.
- Only 24% of Generation DotNet—15- to 25-year-olds—follow government and public affairs "very often," compared with 60% of pre-baby boomer voters, 50% of baby boomers, and 37% of GenXers.
- The number one reason **people don't vote is because they feel their vote won't matter.** Other reasons include too much negative campaigning, the sense that the political parties are too similar, **an overall disgust with politics, and a lack of good candidates.**

71 million eligible voters didn't vote in the 2004 presidential election.

TAKE ACTION TODAY

1. **Register to vote** by using the National Mail Voter Registration Form. Obtain this form online at rockthevote.com or eac.gov.
2. **Register in person** at your local DMV, state offices providing public assistance or programs for the disabled, official campaign headquarters, armed forces recruitment offices, public libraries, post offices, public high schools, and universities.
3. **Pay attention to the registration deadlines** in your state to ensure that you register in time to vote.
4. Make sure your friends, family, co-workers, or fellow students are registered.
5. Get informed on the issues and candidates.
6. Vote.

YOU MATTER

The numbers don't lie...registered voters vote. Are you registered?

Something Worth Partying For.

party with a purpose

FACTS

Every WEEK there are:
79,623 births
42,884 weddings
5,812,037 birthdays

- **Birthdays are the #1 reason people celebrate.**
- There are millions of other gift-giving/receiving occasions every year, such as bat and bar mitzvahs, graduations, funerals, retirements, and debutante balls.
- **Every year, nearly 140 million people purchase and/or receive a gift card with an average value of $59.**
- $747 is the average amount spent annually on holiday gifts.

TAKE ACTION TODAY

1. Select a charity, cause, or purpose **you wish to support.**
2. Decide which holiday or occasion for which you would like your friends and family to make a **donation instead of giving you a gift.**
3. Provide your friends and family with the proper information to make their giving easier— **Web site, phone number, or address.**
4. If there is not a specific reason for having a party, make one up. Simply have guests bring a food dish or beverage along with money for **your charity of choice or for someone in need.**

YOU MATTER

If everyone gives up their birthday gifts this year, more than **$3 billion dollars** can be donated **to worthy causes or needy people.** Friends and family donating money in your name can be much **more rewarding** than getting material gifts. **Giving** is a lot more gratifying than receiving, **no matter the occasion.**

make today matter...

Donate Books

FACTS

- **61% of low-income families have no books in their homes.**
- 43% of adults with the lowest level of literacy proficiency live in poverty.
- Only 4% of adults with strong literacy skills live in poverty.
- **55% of children have an increased interest in reading when given books at an early age.**
- Children with a greater variety of reading material in the home are more creative, imaginative, and proficient in reading. They are also on a better path toward educational growth and development.
- **There is only 1 age-appropriate book for every 300 children in low-income neighborhoods compared to 13 books per child in middle-income neighborhoods.**

TAKE ACTION TODAY

1. **Go through your bookshelves and pull out books that you will never read again** or have owned for more than 2 years and haven't read yet.
2. Pack the books in a box.
3. Call your local library, school, foster home, or children's organization to see if they need books.
4. **Deliver the books.**
5. If you don't have any books at home, purchase some to donate or find an organization that accepts financial donations and will purchase books and deliver them where they are needed.

YOU MATTER

The majority of children in low-income neighborhoods often lack libraries and bookstores. **Having access to books is the key to literacy. By donating your books,** especially children's books, **you can impact some of the 12 million children** who don't have books at home.

Imagine if you couldn't read this book.

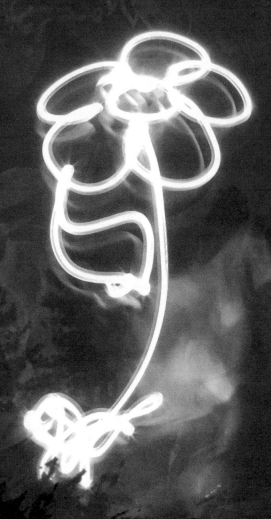

THE DYING ART OF ART.

CREATE, SUPPORT, APPRECIATE ART

FACTS

- **93% of people believe that the arts are vital to a well-rounded education.**
- Regardless, only 29% of schools have been able to maintain time and funding for art programs.
- **Children spend more time at their locker than in art classes.**
- People learn to be more tolerant and open to other people when creating or appreciating art.
- Art promotes individuality, bolsters self-confidence, and improves overall academic performance.
- Art is a reflection of people and cultures since the beginning of time.
- **Students who take 4 years of arts and music in high school average 100 points higher on their SATs than students who took only a half year or less.**

TAKE ACTION TODAY

1. **Create** an original piece of art today. If you don't know how or where to start, visit your local craft store and ask for help.
2. **Sign up** for an art class with a friend.
3. **Visit a local museum**, art gallery, or sculpture garden.
4. **Volunteer to support** an art activity at a local school or senior citizen program.
5. **Communicate** with your school-district administrators or national legislators by either writing a letter of appreciation for current funding or requesting funding for the arts.

YOU MATTER

Sit down with friends and family and TAKE SOME TIME TO BE A KID AGAIN.

With minimal supplies, you can create a unique piece of art and give it to someone as a gift.

If creating art is not your thing, then support the people who do love it by visiting a museum, donating art supplies, buying art from a local artist, or writing a letter to the people who control the school budgets.

Just as there are many ways you can express art, there are also many ways you can support and appreciate it.

TRAFFIC IS OVERRATED.

Rideshare

FACTS

- **Only 10.2% of workers rideshare.**
- 52.5 cents per mile is the average cost to drive a car due to fuel, maintenance, tires, depreciation, and insurance.
- **$2,520 can be saved annually by each person in a 2-person, 40-mile roundtrip rideshare.**
- 12,000 gallons of gasoline would be saved each year for every 100 people who paired up into a daily rideshare.
- **18 pounds of CO_2 is produced by burning 1 gallon of gasoline.**
- A 10% nationwide increase in transit ridership would **save 135 million gallons of gasoline a year.**
- 34% of roads are in poor or mediocre condition due to heavy usage and lack of proper repairs.

Save your car, the roads, and your tax dollars.

TAKE ACTION TODAY

1. **Find a rideshare partner.**
Ask a co-worker, fellow student, or friend.
2. Check with your company or school to see if there is an organized rideshare program.
3. **Follow these guidelines:**
   - Meet new rideshare partner(s) before your first commute.
   - Discuss preferences like seating arrangements, music, eating, cell phone usage, and smoking.
   - Set up a probationary period to try out the arrangement.
   - Provide information about your rideshare partner(s) to someone else in case of emergency.
   - Create an equitable driving and cost arrangement.
   - **Be punctual.**
4. Do something meaningful with the **$2,520 you save**.

YOU MATTER

Ridesharing reduces gasoline usage, vehicle wear, traffic, stress, pollution, and ***dependency on foreign oil.*** With every 100 people who pair up daily and rideshare for a year, we keep 1,848 pounds of hydrocarbons, 1,320 pounds of carbon monoxide, 792 pounds of nitrogen oxides, and 2,376,000 pounds of carbon dioxide from entering the atmosphere.

You might even make a friend or two.

WARNING

NEIGHBORHOOD WATCH
PROGRAM IN FORCE

We immediately report all SUSPICIOUS PERSONS and activities to our Police Dept.

1982 THE SIGN CENTER INC   PO BOX 4087 SAN DIEGO CA 92104

THEY
MISSED
BY ONE
HOUSE

SUPPORT NEIGHBORHOOD WATCH

FACTS

- **Over 3.4 million burglaries occur annually.**
- 60% or more of residential burglaries occur during daylight hours.
- **Every 14.6 seconds a burglary takes place.**
- Over 60% of all burglaries are by forcible entry by breaking windows, and forcing open doors, windows, or locks.
- **Approximately 32% of all burglaries are by unlawful entry with no force: the robbers enter via an open door or window.**
- The average loss per residential burglary is $1,725.
- July has the greatest number of burglaries; February, the least.
- **Only 17%, or 1 in 6 people, volunteer in a program that prevents crime.**

YOU MATTER

A safe neighborhood is created when the people who live in the community look out for one another and their property. Keeping a watchful eye, noticing and reporting unusual activities, and talking with neighbors to make them aware of neighborhood happenings all help create a crime watch program and a safe community.

TAKE ACTION TODAY

1. Get to know your neighbors.
2. Organize a community watch program to protect your neighborhood. Obtain training and necessary information from your local law enforcement agency.
3. Post a Neighborhood Watch sign in a visible window of your home and encourage neighbors to do the same.
4. Ask neighbors to be observant and report suspicious or unusual activities.
5. Let your neighbors know when you'll be out of town and leave a contact number where you can be reached.
6. Make your home safer by installing an alarm system, placing rods in the frames of sliding windows and doors, leaving outdoor lights (CFLs) on at night, setting indoor lamps with timers, and **adopting a dog.**

LET'S MAKE IT MORE DIFFICULT FOR BURGLARS TO DO THEIR JOB.

THERE IS NO REASON TWO LIVES NEED TO BE LOST
lung
heart
lung
liver
pancreas
tissue
kidney
kidney

DONATE your ORGANS

Register to

FACTS

- **Over 97,000 people are in need of one or more organs.**
- 77 people receive organ transplants every day.
- **There is no age limit on who can donate.**
- 300 new transplant candidates are added to the waiting list each month.
- **Most family members are not aware of one another's willingness to be a donor, even if it is indicated on their driver's license.**

TAKE ACTION TODAY

1. Declare on your driver's license your wish to donate tissue and organs.
2. **Carry a donor card in your wallet.**
3. Sign up on your state's donor registry today.
4. **Inform your family, loved ones, and physician of your decision.**

YOU MATTER

EIGHTEEN PEOPLE DIE EVERY DAY WAITING FOR A TRANSPLANT

Because more people need transplants than there are organs available, register your organs on the donor registry. In addition to indicating your wishes on your driver's license, make your family members aware of your decision. Saving a life by donating a heart, lung, or kidney or allowing someone to see again through your cornea may be the most significant gift you ever give...
and you may not even be aware you are giving it.

If you can't FEED a
hundred PEOPLE,

then just feed ONE.

- Mother Teresa

Big things come in small packages.

Show Your Smile

FACTS

- A smile is a universal expression of happiness and recognized as such by all cultures.
- **A smiling person is judged to be more pleasant, attractive, sincere, sociable, and competent.**
- Smiling or even seeing somebody smile releases endorphins that work in the brain to give an overall feeling of well-being.
- Happy people generally don't get sick as often as people who are unhappy.
- **People are born with the ability to smile. Even babies born blind smile.**
- Adults laugh approximately 15 times per day, while children laugh about 400 times a day.
- It takes only 17 muscles to smile compared to 43 muscles to frown.
- **Women smile more than men.**

TAKE ACTION TODAY

1. Smile at EVERYONE you see today.
2. Keep track of how many times you smile and laugh today.
3. If you are having trouble smiling, here are a few suggestions to help:
- Make faces at yourself in the mirror.
- Shake your body like it's laughing from inside.
- Jump on the bed.
- Hug someone you love.
- Visit a pet store.

4. At the end of **your day of smiling,** notice how you feel and whether people acted differently around you.

Smiling is contagious.

YOU MATTER

Happiness leads to smiling, and smiling leads to **h a p p i n e s s .** Happiness is your natural immunity, having a profound, positive effect on your health and **w e l l - b e i n g .** **If you are happy, smile.** If you aren't happy, smile anyway. **It will help you get there.**

THEY GIVE MORE THAN THEY TAKE.

ADOPT A PET

FACTS

- **There are 4,000 to 6,000 animal shelters.**
- Nearly 8 million dogs and cats are placed in shelters each year.
- **Approximately 4 million dogs and cats are euthanized each year because not enough people want them.**
- 1 out of 4 dogs in shelters are purebreds. Adoption fees are usually much less than the cost of purchasing dogs from pet stores and breeders.
- **Only 16% of owned dogs and 15% of owned cats were adopted from an animal shelter.**
- Many shelters vaccinate, deworm, and spay or neuter for free.

TAKE ACTION TODAY

1. Go to a shelter near you to see if there is an animal with which you "connect." If not, visit another shelter or return another day.

2. Speak with an adoption counselor at the shelter about whether your choice of a particular type or breed will be best for you.

3. Only select a pet if you have a realistic understanding of the time, effort, and money required to provide a healthy, loving environment for your pet.

4. Enjoy your newfound friend.

YOU MATTER

Animals are unconcerned about age, looks, or physical ability; they accept you just as you are. If you're **thinking about getting a pet, seriously consider adopting.** Not only will you be saving your new pet's life, but you'll also be rewarded with years of companionship, entertainment, unconditional love, and increased opportunities to meet others.

SINGLE? GO TO A DOG PARK... BUT ONLY IF YOU HAVE A DOG.

Don't Flick Your Cigarette Butt

FACTS

- **The average smoker smokes 10,000 cigarettes a year.**
- Cigarette butts are the most commonly littered item.
- **Over 100 billion cigarette butts weighing 100 million pounds end up as litter each year.**
- Cigarette filters are made of cellulose acetate, a plastic that takes decades to decompose.
- **25% of all ocean and beach debris is cigarette butts.**
  They have been found in the stomachs of fish, birds, whales, and other marine creatures that mistake them for food.
- **Over 750 civilian deaths, 1,500 critical injuries, and $480 million in direct property damage**
  occur each year due to over 25,000 cigarette-caused fires.

**Annual cigarette butt litter, end on end, measures more than 2 million miles.
That's 337 roundtrips from Los Angeles to New York.**

TAKE ACTION TODAY

1. If you smoke today, don't litter the butt.

2. When you see a friend, neighbor, co-worker, or stranger smoking, ask him or her to discard the butt in an appropriate receptacle.

3. If you see someone flick a cigarette butt on the ground, politely ask them to pick it up, or do it yourself.
Maybe they will see you and get the point.

4. Consider posting the above statistics at designated smoking areas at your workplace or school.

5. Utilize a pocket ashtray or purchase one for someone who smokes.

6. Don't smoke.

YOU MATTER

Why is it that people who wouldn't even **think about throwing trash** into the street **don't hesitate** to flick a cigarette butt? Most people who litter their cigarettes either don't fully understand the consequences of their actions or they have rationalized their behavior. Imagine fewer fires as well as less litter, pollution, and harm to animals simply because people stopped throwing their cigarette butts out their car window or tossing them on the ground.
The sheer volume of **cigarette butt litter isn't just ugly...** **it's hazardous.**

CPR
AIRWAY
BREATHING
CIRCULATION

THE
A, B, Cs
OF LIFE.

LEARN CPR

FACTS

- Cardiac arrest may be caused by drowning, drug overdoses, poisoning, electrocution, and many other conditions.
- **95% of sudden cardiac arrest victims die before reaching the hospital.**
- 75 to 80% of all out-of-hospital cardiac arrests **happen at home.**
- **4 to 6 minutes after someone experiences cardiac arrest, brain death starts to occur.**
- CPR helps maintain vital blood flow to the heart and brain and increases the amount of time that an electric shock from a defibrillator can be effective.

TAKE ACTION TODAY

1. Call your local hospital to find a place near you that teaches CPR or to arrange for a certified CPR instructor to come to your school or workplace.

2. Sign up for a class with a family member, friend, or even your kids.

3. Learn CPR. It only takes a few hours.

4. Post CPR guidelines in a kitchen cupboard, your office, your car, and anywhere else you frequent. These guidelines may come in handy **during emergency situations.** Tell people around you that the guidelines are there in case they need to perform CPR.

CPR CAN DOUBLE A VICTIM'S CHANCE OF SURVIVAL.

YOU MATTER

What if you could have saved a life had you known CPR?
What if you needed help and no one around you could help you?
Take a few hours today to learn this life-saving skill.
It can change your life—and someone else's life—forever.

They fight the good fight
...oftentimes for free.

Thank a Firefighter

FACTS

- There are over **1,100,000 firefighters.**
- 73% of firefighters are volunteers, with 66% or more of fire departments staffed 100% by volunteers.
- More than **100 firefighters die in the line of duty each year.**
- **1.5 million** or more fires are reported annually.
- Fire kills more Americans than all natural disasters combined, with over **4,000 deaths annually.**
- The **U.S. has one of the highest rates of death due to fire** in the industrialized world.

TAKE ACTION TODAY

1. When you see firefighters in uniform, walk up and thank them for keeping you and your community safe.
2. Get out of the way.
Pull your car to the right when you hear a siren or see a fire truck with its lights on.
3. Organize your friends, co-workers, neighborhood, or child's class to create and **deliver a thank-you card to your local fire station.**
4. Donate to firefighter benefits and causes.
If you don't know of any, ask your local fire department which organizations support them.
5. Minimize your risk of fires—install smoke detectors, keep a fire extinguisher in your kitchen, don't overload power plugs, clear brush from around your house, and don't flick your cigarette butts.

YOU MATTER

Every day firefighters **put their lives on the line** to save people and property. Many of these firefighters are volunteers, so let's "pay" them by showing our appreciation, thanking them for the valuable service they provide, and letting them know that we are very aware of the **significant positive impact** they have on our communities. Firefighters, whether paid or not, make an incredible difference in our lives **so let's make a difference in theirs.**

No
one
is
immune.

Get Tested

FACTS

- **The U.S. has the highest rate of sexually transmitted diseases (STDs)** in the industrialized world, with over 65 million people infected.
- 19 million new cases of STDs are diagnosed every year.
- **1 in 4 teens contracts an STD each year.**
- **1 in 2 sexually active persons under the age of 25** will contract an STD.
- Over $14 billion is spent each year to diagnose and treat STDs, excluding HIV.
- Nearly **1 million people are estimated to have HIV**, and 25% are *unaware* of their infection.
- 50% of the population will likely have an STD at some point in their lifetime.

STDs and HIV are preventable.

TAKE ACTION TODAY

1. Call your physician or locate a testing facility near you and make an appointment to get tested for STDs and HIV. *Testing is anonymous and can be free of charge.*
2. Get the information you need before getting tested. Counseling and support are available to help assess your risks and understand your results.
3. If your test results are negative and *you are sexually active, use a condom*. Abstinence is *always the safest policy*.
4. If you test positive, be responsible: get treated and tell your intimate partner. *Be honest and give full disclosure.*
5. Don't use drugs. If you do, don't share the needle.

YOU MATTER

We need to take responsibility for transmitting infections and diseases to others. *Save lives, money, heartache, and emotional burden by getting tested.* *If you could prevent* yourself from passing along a life-threatening infection, disease, or inconvenience to *someone,* wouldn't you?

DON'T HONK

FACTS

- **Noise is among the most pervasive pollutants today.**
- 28 million people have impaired hearing caused by noise.
- **Hearing loss is occurring in people at younger and younger ages.**
- Overexposure to noise can cause increased heart rate, respiration, sweating, headaches, stress, blood pressure, and sleep loss.
- The law states that a driver of a motor vehicle, when reasonably necessary to ensure safe operation, shall give audible warning with the horn. The law prohibits the use of horns for any other reason, except as part of an alarm system.
- **Sound is measured by decibels (dBA). Common sounds include normal conversation (60 dBA), a noisy restaurant (85 dBA), a car horn (110 dBA), and a jackhammer (130 dBA).**
- At 110 dBA, the maximum exposure time is 1 minute and 29 seconds before hearing damage can occur.

Noise-induced hearing loss, though preventable, is permanent.

TAKE ACTION TODAY

1. Only use your horn when it is reasonably necessary to ensure the safe operation of your vehicle.
2. Don't use your horn
to let someone know you're angry,
to tell people you're waiting
outside to pick them up,
to say good-bye,
and/or as a way of protesting.
3. Get your hearing checked.

YOU MATTER

You can be both the cause and the victim of noise. Noise-induced hearing loss is cumulative over one's lifespan. To avoid noise-induced hearing loss, pay attention to the noises around you, turn down the volume whenever possible, and don't honk your horn unnecessarily. Often, by the time you realize you are losing your hearing, it's too late.

WHAT?

Air. Water. Beauty. Green.

Plant a Tree

FACTS

- **1 acre of trees produces enough oxygen for 18 people every day.**
- Planting trees remains one of the most cost-effective means of drawing excess CO_2 from the atmosphere. 1 acre of trees can absorb the same amount of CO_2 produced by a car driven 26,000 miles.
- **3 trees planted strategically around a house can reduce energy use by up to 50%.**
- Trees add beauty, increase property values, and reduce stress.
- **1 tree planted by every family would reduce 1 billion pounds of CO_2 annually from our atmosphere.**

TAKE ACTION TODAY

1. **Call your local nursery** to get a list of trees that grow best in your area; then determine the type of tree you would like to plant.
2. **To plant the tree:**
   - Identify the proper location.
   - Dig a hole at least twice as big as the root ball of the tree.
   - Place several inches of good soil mix at the bottom of the hole before inserting the tree.
   - Place the tree in the hole. If your tree comes in a plastic pot, burlap, or wire basket, remove it from the container without disturbing the root system.
   - Fill the hole with **good soil** and pack firmly.
   - Anchor your tree using a tree stake. Use wire and a length of old hose to secure tree to the stake—the hose will keep the wire from cutting through the trunk. Remove anchor after two years.
   - Water thoroughly and fertilize as directed.
3. **Give a tree to someone as a gift.**

YOU MATTER

Trees improve our air quality, save energy, reduce pollutants, provide homes for wildlife, and add brilliant colors to landscapes. Planting 100 million trees can reduce the amount of carbon by an estimated 18 million tons per year and, at the same time, save consumers $4 billion each year on utility bills. **100 million trees—that's the goal.**

So get out your shovel.

Putting
the world
back
together
again.

Support a Global Cause

FACTS

In the world:
- Every **3.5 seconds** someone dies of hunger.
- Every **11 seconds** someone dies of AIDS.
- Every **15 seconds** a child dies from a waterborne illness.

- **40 million people are living with HIV/AIDS.**
- **1 billion** have no access to clean water.
- **2.6 billion** live without basic sanitation.
- **5 million** live in refugee camps.
- **1.08 billion** live on **$1 or less per day.**
- **2 million** children die each year from diseases that inexpensive vaccines could have prevented.
- **11 million children die before they reach their 5th birthday.** That's as if every child under five living in the United Kingdom, France, and Germany were to die in a single year.
- **Enough food is produced to feed everyone.**
- Every year more than 16 million people—the equivalent of one hundred 747 jets crashing every day of the year—die from:

  Hunger 9,125,000
  HIV/AIDS 2,900,000
  Pneumonia 2,000,000
  Diarrhea 1,600,000
  Malaria 1,000,000

YOU MATTER

The numbers are unbelievable, but they reflect a truth we cannot ignore. This is OUR world. You, your friends, your family, your co-workers ALL matter when it comes to changing the statistics. Each one of you can make a huge difference. Every day we put off helping our world, we lose tens of thousands of people... **many of whom died while you were reading this page.**

TAKE ACTION TODAY

1. Pick a global organization that interests you. The needs are many and obvious.
2. Get involved TODAY.

Poverty is the common denominator.

ARE YOU STILL UNIQUE?

Protect Yourself from IDENTITY THEFT

FACTS

- **8.4 million adults are victims of identity fraud annually.**
- Over $50 billion is stolen from victims of identity theft every year.
- **$5,720 is the average fraud amount per victim.**
- 25 hours per victim is the average time required to resolve identity theft and its consequences.
- **$6,270 is the average amount lost by people ages 25–34, the group that experiences the highest rate of identity fraud at 5.4%.**
- 63% of identity information is obtained through traditional methods, such as lost or stolen wallets; misappropriation by family, friends, co-workers, and neighbors; and stolen mail or trash.

YOU MATTER

When someone steals your name, *social security number, and credit,* **they steal YOU.** *Victims of identity theft may lose job opportunities, be refused loans for housing, cars, and education, and even get arrested for crimes they didn't commit. Taking simple measures to protect yourself can save you time, money, credit damage, frustration, anger, and possibly humiliation.* **You protect your personal belongings,**

TAKE ACTION TODAY

1. **Use a paper shredder for important documents like credit applications, credit offers, insurance forms, physician statements, bank statements, and expired charge cards.**
2. Deposit outgoing mail in collection boxes located inside the post office.
3. Promptly remove mail from your home or business mailbox.
4. Don't carry your Social Security card with you.
5. Keep personal information in a safe and secure location at home.
6. Don't give out personal information on the phone, through the mail, or on the Internet unless you've initiated the contact or are sure you know with whom you are dealing.
7. Create passwords that are random combinations of numbers, symbols, and both upper- and lowercase letters.
8. Order a free copy of your credit report every 12 months.
9. Check your online bank statement on a regular basis.

WHY NOT PROTECT YOUR IDENTITY?

THE BILLION DOLLAR KILLER.

NO FAST FOOD

monday
28

FACTS

- $120+ billion is spent every year on fast food, compared to $6 billion in 1970.
- **30% of children's meals consist of fast food.**
- 24% of high schools offer popular fast-food brands.
- **1 in 5 children between the ages of 6 and 17 are overweight.**
- There is a 79% likelihood of adult obesity if a person is overweight during adolescence.
- **Large portions, value meals, and supersizing create serving sizes that are double and triple the recommended daily allowance.**
- Billions of dollars are spent each year on fast food advertising specifically targeted at children.

TAKE ACTION TODAY

1. Don't eat fast food today.
2. Start the habit of switching one fast food meal per week to a healthier alternative.
3. On days you do eat fast food, ask for the small size.
4. Never supersize your meal. **The price and value may be tempting, but your health pays the greatest price.**
5. Plan your meals at least a few days in advance.
6. Go to the store and buy fresh or organic food.
7. Pack a healthy lunch or cook dinner at home today.

YOU MATTER

With each fast-food feast, you significantly increase your carbohydrate and fat intake as well as the calories you eat. So plan your meals, simplify your schedule, cook, and eat dinner as a family. Fast food may save you minutes in your day, but it's **taking years off your life...** **most chains don't advertise that on their "value" menu.**

The power of the pencil.

Write a Note of Gratitude

F - Every week, the average person receives:
   682 e-mails   12 text messages   10.8 pieces of junk mail   1.5 personal letters
A - Feeling appreciated is one of the **strongest human desires.**
C - There is warmth in a handwritten note—it instantly makes the message more personal,
   creates a more intimate feeling, and makes the recipient feel more valued.
T - With e-mail and instant messaging, a handwritten note is getting rarer and therefore more special.
S - A handwritten note costs less than a dollar to write and mail, and the relational value is priceless.
   - **The recipient can keep and reread it forever.**

TAKE ACTION TODAY

1. Select the person—a family member, friend, co-worker, or someone you haven't spoken to in a long time—whom you want to **thank for what he or she brings to your life.**
2. Choose a postcard, letter, or card.
3. Take a few minutes to write a warm, sincere message that clearly communicates **your love and appreciation** for that person.
4. Decide if you want to add any special touches like unique paper, scents, photographs, drawings on the envelope, or a specialty stamp. *Send It Today.*

YOU MATTER

*How many e-mails or text messages have you sent in the past week? How many handwritten notes of appreciation? More to the point, when was the last time you handwrote anything to anyone? Handwrite a note of gratitude to somebody today...**just because.** **They will appreciate the rarity of it.***

It's more than
just pencils and paper.

Create a Back-to-School Backpack

FACTS

- **28 million children from low-income families enter school each fall.**
- Children need school supplies to do their schoolwork and homework.
- **Required school supplies cost between $20 and $100,** depending on the grade level. This expense can be a financial burden for low-income families, especially those with more than one child.
- Having new and proper school supplies increases a child's confidence, self-esteem, and excitement about school.
- **Children who feel good about themselves and their abilities are much more likely to do well in school—and in life.**

TAKE ACTION TODAY

1. Select a family in your neighborhood or workplace who is in financial need and has school-aged children. Or call a local elementary school, soup kitchen, or church to find a family.

2. Get your friends, co-workers, and family members involved so you can buy in bulk. It's more cost-effective, and more kids can benefit.

3. Go to the Web site of the child's school to see if a list of supplies for each grade level is posted.

4. If nothing is listed on the school's Web site, here are some items you could include:

One school backpack	One pencil box or pencil bag
Six #2 pencils	Two-pocket paper folders
Six medium ballpoint pens	Two wide-ruled spiral notebooks
One package of colored pencils	One package of notebook paper
One package of markers	One 12-inch ruler
One barrel pencil sharpener	Calculator

5. Select backpacks and school supplies that are fun and gender specific.

6. Deliver the backpacks with a smile.

YOU MATTER

Both a child's performance in school and self-esteem can impact their entire life, as well as the community in which they grow up. Help make going back to school a positive experience by purchasing and stocking a backpack for a child.

Not only are you eliminating a challenge for a low-income family, you are enabling a young student to start the school year on a more level playing field.

Treat the Homeless with Dignity

FACTS

- 2.3 to 3.5 million people are homeless at some point each year.
- 750,000 people sleep on the streets every night.
- 30% of the homeless are families with children, and 71% are single-parent families—the fastest growing group of all homeless.
- 44% of the homeless population has part- or full-time employment.
- Less than 30% of those eligible for low-income housing actually receive it because of a nationwide lack of affordable housing and assisted-housing programs.
- Contrary to public perception, only 22% of the single adult homeless suffer from some form of severe and ongoing mental illness.
- 94% of the nation's homeless do not want to be homeless.

TAKE ACTION TODAY

1. **Don't judge** people based on their outward appearances or life circumstances.
2. Better understand who the homeless are by talking to them on the street or by volunteering to serve food at a mission, shelter, or soup kitchen. You'll be surprised by what you learn.
3. Look a homeless person in the eye, show consideration, be polite, and smile. Simply say "hello" or "God bless you." **They are human, just like you.**
4. Instead of money, offer bottled water, ready-to-eat food, or toiletries.
5. If a homeless person asks for help and you are not able to, rather than treating them with indifference or ignoring them, simply state, **"I'm sorry. I'm not able to help today."**

YOU MATTER

People don't want to be homeless. Yet millions of people may only be one missed paycheck, one health crisis, or **one unpaid bill away from becoming homeless.** How many paychecks can you miss and still afford to pay the rent or mortgage? **Treat the homeless with dignity and respect;** they are not that different from you.

FACTS

- **The #1 killer of people ages 4 to 37 is car accidents.**
- Over 43,000 people die in car accidents each year, and 2.7 million are injured.
- **1 in 5 drivers under the age of 30 is stopped for speeding every year.**
- 75% of drivers admit to driving over the speed limit, and 50% determine their speed based on the chance of being stopped by police.
- **6.1 million motor vehicle crashes are reported to police each year.**
- 30% of all traffic fatalities have speed as a factor, second only to alcohol (39%) as a cause of fatal crashes.
- With every 10-mph increase in speeds above 50 mph, the impact of the force of the crash is doubled.
- **The annual cost of speed-related crashes is $40.4 billion.**

TAKE ACTION TODAY

1. Obey speed limit signs. Doing so shows *respect for the law, your life, and the lives of others.*
2. Slow down to give yourself time to avoid hitting debris, animals, and potholes. Potholes cause *millions of dollars in damage* to cars each year.
3. Stay at least one car length behind the vehicle in front of you for every 10 mph you're driving.
4. **Leave early. Allow enough time to get where you're going.**
5. Use caution and take appropriate safety measures when driving in extreme weather conditions.

YOU MATTER

You can't get a speeding ticket if you don't speed.
It costs you nothing to slow down, and you'll even save money on gas and brakes.
You also set a good example for other motorists and for anyone who is in the car with you.

The accident you prevent or the life you save just may be your own.

Learn, Grow, Escape...

Read a Book

FACTS

- Only **1 in 6 people** read 12 or more books a year.
- Fewer than half of today's adults are literary readers, meaning they read novels, mysteries, contemporary and classic fiction, short stories, plays, or poetry.
- Leisure reading has declined 7% over the last 10 years for both genders and all ethnicities, education levels, and ages.
- **55% of women read** for leisure compared to 37% of men.
- 43% of all literary readers **perform volunteer and charity work** compared to 17% of non-literary readers. The more books people read, the more active and involved they are in their communities.
- **Book buying constitutes less than 6%** of total recreational spending while spending on music, videos, computers, and software constitutes roughly 25%.

TAKE ACTION TODAY

1. Read a book you've never read before. If you don't have one on your shelf, go to the library or local bookstore, or order one online.
2. Join a book club or start one with your friends or co-workers.
3. Give books to people as gifts...especially this one!

YOU MATTER

Reading is like exercising—mental and physical benefits flourish with regular practice. Reading **improves language skills**, vocabulary, and spelling skills; it introduces **new ideas, perspectives, and information**; it staves off the effects of aging by keeping your mind active; it provides a vehicle for mental escape and creativity; and it relaxes, entertains, and inspires your soul.

Take time out to read today...this page doesn't count.

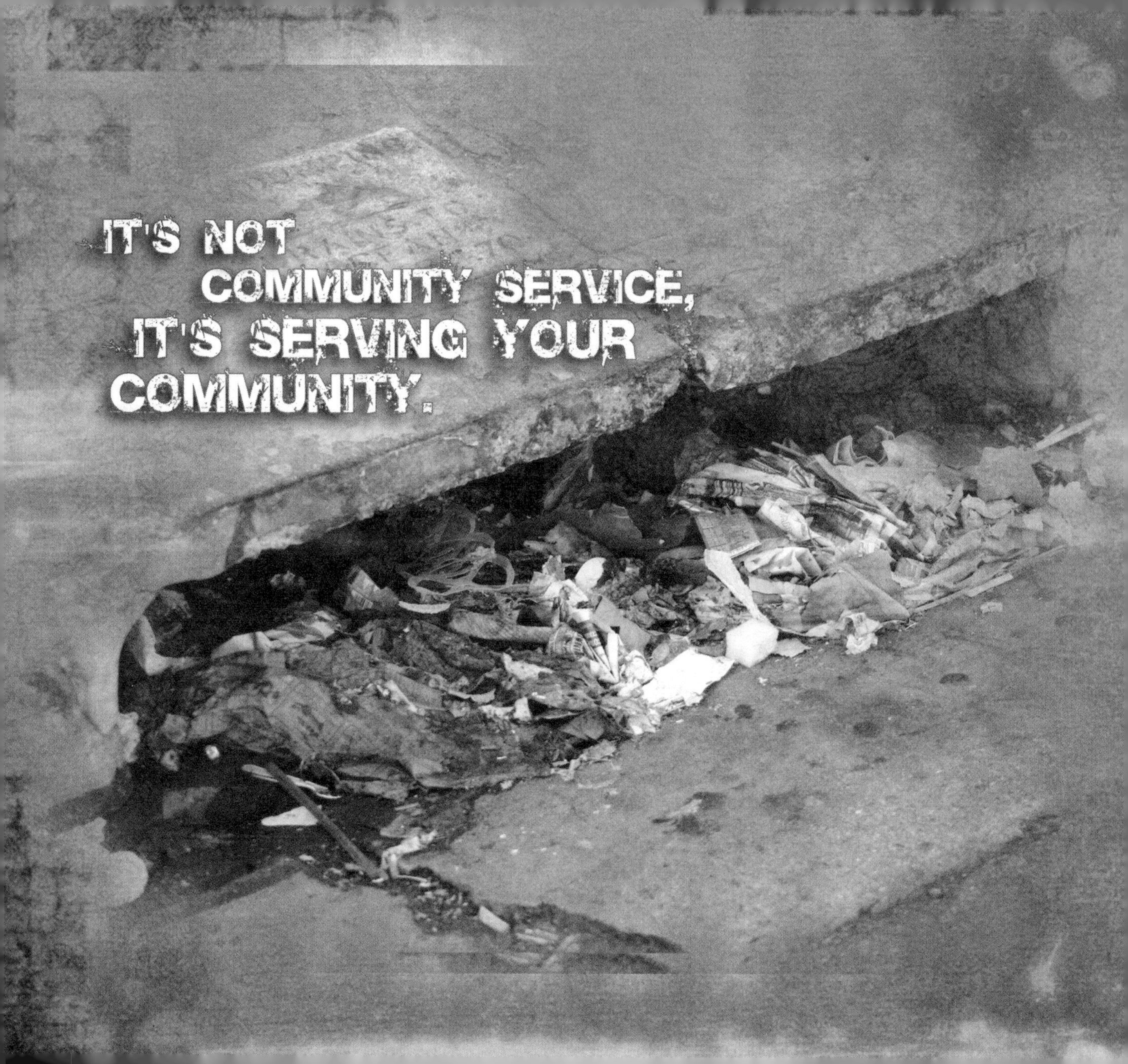
IT'S NOT
COMMUNITY SERVICE,
IT'S SERVING YOUR
COMMUNITY.

PICK UP LITTER

FACTS

- **180 million tons of trash** is generated every year.
- Common litter includes cigarette butts, plastic bags, paper, candy wrappers, fast-food packaging, bottle caps, 6-pack can holders, glass bottles, and plastic straws.
- Men and women are equally likely to litter.
- **People under age 15 are least likely to litter**; people under the age of 25 are most likely to litter when in a group; and people over the age of 25 are most likely to litter when alone.
- **In one single day nearly 7 million pounds of litter** were removed from beaches, lakes, and streams.
- **Animals from nearly 300 species** die from ingesting or getting entangled in marine debris annually.
- People litter because they:
  - **Don't think** of the item as litter.
  - **View litter** removal as someone else's responsibility.
  - **Lack knowledge** about the environmental effects of their littering.

TAKE ACTION TODAY

1. Spend **one hour** today picking up litter. Or decide that every time you see a piece of litter today, you'll pick it up and **throw it away.**

2. If you see someone litter, politely ask them to **pick it up**. Or pick it up yourself and maybe the person who dropped it will see you and get the hint.

3. Organize a team of neighbors, friends, co-workers, or fellow church members to pick up litter in a specific neighborhood for an hour. Bring rubber gloves and garbage bags and make it more fun by **turning the cleanup effort into a game/contest.**

4. Enjoy making a difference, getting exercise, getting to know people better, and having **cleaner surroundings.**

YOU MATTER

If every person picked up **just one piece of litter today**, there would be over 300 million fewer pieces of litter. If every person picked up 10 pieces of litter, there would be 3 billion fewer pieces damaging our environment. If you and your friends **spend just one hour today** picking up litter in your own neighborhood, you will not only pick up thousands of pieces of trash, you will also make a tremendous impact on your community.

JUST BE SURE TO BEND YOUR KNEES.

Be the CHANGE

you wish to see
in the WORLD.

- Mahatma Gandhi

make it happen.

GOEXERCISE

FACTS

- **More than 50% of adults do not get enough physical activity and 24% are not physically active at all.**
- 1 death occurs every 36 seconds from heart disease and strokes.
- **Over 18% of children and 66% of adults are overweight, with 32.9% being obese.**
- Over 100 million adults have above normal or high cholesterol levels.
- **Roughly 20 million people have depressive disorders.**
- 1 in 3 adults has high blood pressure.

TAKE ACTION TODAY

1. Set a goal for yourself. Think about what types of benefits you want to achieve.
Weight loss? Increased muscle mass? Improved general health?
2. Figure out what type of exercise you like most and best suits your desired goal.
3. Create a plan. Start with 3 days a week, 30 minutes per day. Try to build up to 4 or 5 days a week, 45 minutes per day.
4. Drink plenty of water before, during, and after exercising.
5. Don't buy into excuses like "I don't have enough time" and "I can't afford a gym membership."
6. Incorporate exercise into your workday by taking the stairs,
walking during your lunch break, and stretching while at your desk.
7. Always consult a physician or exercise specialist for safety and guidance.

YOU MATTER

Do you really want to have heart disease, high blood pressure, a stroke, lung disease,
diabetes, high cholesterol, osteoporosis, depression, arthritis, or unwanted pounds?
If not, start incorporating regular physical activity into your day. By doing so, you'll increase your overall health,
well-being, and quality of life. Physical activity does not need to be painful in order to be beneficial,

so put this book down and go get some.

Just walk out your front door.

Be Neighborly

F A C T S

- The average dual-career couple works away from their home a combined 18.2 hours a day.
- **Urban sprawl is creating longer commutes—approximately 25 minutes per day.**
- People spend less than 15 minutes per day doing outside chores and gardening compared to over **3 hours watching TV or movies and surfing on the Internet.**
- The average person or family has friends over for dinner about 45% less often than they did in the 70s.
- In 1926, the first electric automated garage door opener was invented by C. G. Johnson, beginning the drive-in-and-shut-the-door method of entering your home.
- **The increased number of fenced backyards, coupled with the disappearance of front porches and verandas, has privatized residences more than ever.**

TAKE ACTION TODAY

1. Meet a neighbor you've never met before. Simply knock on the door and introduce yourself. Take over something you've baked or grown in your garden, or invite them to your house for a beverage or a snack.
2. Make yourself more available to your neighbors.
3. Mow your front lawn, wash your car, go for a walk, or play with your children outside. Or, if you see neighbors doing the same, go out and visit.
4. Plan a neighborhood yard sale or block party.
5. Write a quarterly neighborhood newsletter.

YOU MATTER

Does your mailman know your neighbors better than you do?
It's not enough to just drive by and wave to neighbors from your car window. To get to know your neighbors, you need to have personal interaction with them. But these days, people spend more time indoors watching TV and surfing the Internet than they do outside playing catch, taking walks, and talking to their neighbors. **Change that pattern... be counterculture.**

Remember, you have to be a good neighbor to have a good neighbor.

THE
FACE
OF
OUR
FUTURE

MENTOR A CHILD

FACTS

- **3 million children** are currently enrolled in a mentoring program.
- **15 million youth** are in need of mentoring. If they don't get it, they're more likely to not reach adulthood successfully. These youth are:
  - **73%** more likely to begin using alcohol
  - **63%** more likely to skip a class
  - **54%** more likely to begin using illegal drugs
  - **48%** more likely to skip school
- Mentors **help children develop self-confidence**, relationship skills, and a positive attitude toward school.
- Nearly **70% of inner-city 4th-graders are unable to read** at a basic level.
- **1 out of 3** public high-school students won't graduate.
- Nearly 3 million youth ages 12–15 are at risk of suicide annually, and over 35% will actually attempt suicide—**approximately 2,700 attempts per day.**

TAKE ACTION TODAY

1. Find a mentoring program near you and **apply to become a mentor.**
2. Most mentoring programs will pair you with a child based on your skill set and the child's needs.
3. If you have your own children or know children who could use a mentor, be a self-starter **and create your own mentoring program.**
4. Once a week, spend an hour or two with your mentee doing everyday activities like homework, playing sports, and **having simple conversation.**
5. Set goals with your mentee and **share in the excitement of their achievement and growth.**

YOU MATTER

Children are just as **capable of doing great things** as any other person, but many times they are not equipped with the right foundation, knowledge, encouragement, and **tools to make the right choices.** The decisions they make can **change the entire course of their future.** You may not know what to say or do, but you will quickly realize that

WHAT MATTERS MOST IS THAT YOU CARE.

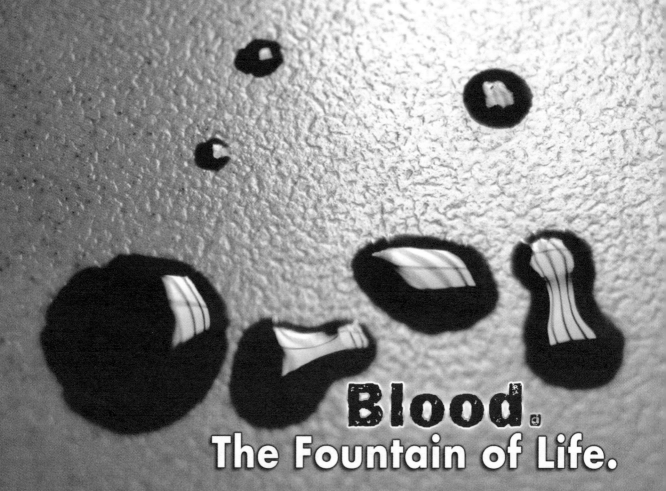

Blood. [cj]
The Fountain of Life.

make today matter...

Donate Blood

FACTS

- **Every 2 seconds someone needs blood.**
- **38,000 pints of blood** are used every day.
- Demand for blood is rising faster than the rate of donations. In fact, donations are declining.
- **1 pint of blood can save up to 3 lives—maybe even the life of someone you know.**
- **60% of the population is eligible to donate**, but less than 5% do on a yearly basis.
- **The #1 reason donors say they give is because they "want to help others."**
- Anyone who is in good health, is at least 17 years old, and weighs at least 110 pounds may **donate blood once every 56 days.**

TAKE ACTION TODAY

1. Find a blood donor location near you and **schedule an appointment today.**
2. Donate blood. The blood **donation process takes approximately 30 minutes.**
3. When you donate, you'll receive a donor card stating your blood type. Keep the card in your wallet.
4. Put yourself on a **regular donating schedule** of once every 56 days. If you have type **O-negative blood**, the universal donor type, your blood is especially needed because it can be **used in emergencies.**

YOU MATTER

Human blood is precious and can't be manufactured outside of the body.
If you gave blood 4 times a year for the next 10 years, you would save 120 lives.
Think of how many lives you could save if you gave blood for the rest of your life!
Saving just one life should be convincing enough.

There is no substitute for human blood.

Have Fun with an Elderly Person

FACTS

- **The fastest growing age group is 85 years and older.**
- Every 7.5 seconds a baby boomer turns 60.
- **1 out of 5 people, or 72 million,** will be 65 years or older by 2030.
- **Nearly 23% of people aged 75 and older live in nursing homes.**
- Due to the increase in divorce rates, a decrease in the number of children, and more family members living farther away from one another, family support for the elderly is less available.

YOU MATTER

Our senior-citizen population is changing— *and this group will grow by another 18 million people in the next 25 years. Today, **seniors are living longer**, **are more full of life**, have more expendable income, and have achieved higher levels of education.*
So, if you spend time with them, you might just find that a friendly game of gin rummy or bingo

will teach you a thing or two ...about life.

TAKE ACTION TODAY

1. Offer the elderly you see today simple gestures of courtesy and respect—smile and say "hello," let them have the right of way while driving, or give up your seat in a crowded area.
2. **Contact a local independent living, assisted living, or continued care facility and ask if they need volunteers.**
3. Ask the facility if children or pets are allowed.
4. **Organize your family or a group of friends to go with you.**
5. Be prepared. Volunteering at a senior or elderly care home can involve many types of activities—playing games or cards, reading, doing art and craft projects, singing songs, teaching a class, or just being friendly.
6. **Ask the seniors questions about their life.**
7. Have fun!

WOULD YOU RISK YOUR LIFE FOR A
TOTAL STRANGER?

THANK A LOCAL
LAWENFORCEMENTOFFICER

FACTS

- **Over 675,000 sworn officers and nearly 295,000 civilian officers protect and serve citizens.**
- Over 14 million arrests occur annually for all offenses except traffic violations.
- Each year:
  - Over 50,000 officers are assaulted while performing their duties.
  - Over 100 are killed—their average age is 37.
  - Over 23 million people are victimized by violent and property crimes.
- **There has been a 58% decline in violent crimes and a 52% decline in property crimes over the last 12 years.**

TAKE ACTION TODAY

1. Walk up and thank a law enforcement officer for keeping you and your community safe.
2. **Pull your car to your right and out of the way when you hear a siren or see a police car approaching with its lights on.**
3. Organize your friends, co-workers, neighborhood, or child's classroom to create and deliver a thank-you card to your local law enforcement agency, police station, or town sheriff.
4. Ask your local police department which organizations support them...and donate.
5. Support or start a Neighborhood Watch program in your community.
6. **Always report crime.**

YOU MATTER

Law enforcement officers make an incredible difference in your community. Every day **they put their lives on the line** to protect you, your neighbors, and your loved ones. Show appreciation, **thank them for their valuable service**, and tell them the impact they have on the lives of the people in your community. Maybe the next officer who pulls you over will be the one to whom you gave **the thank-you note**...

JUST A THOUGHT.

PAPER
OR PLASTIC?

CHOOSE CANVAS BAGS

FACTS

- Almost 7 billion paper bags and 400 billion plastic bags are used every year.
- 90% of all grocery bags are plastic.
- **Only 5.2% of plastic bags and 21% of paper bags are recycled.**
- The average length of time a high-density plastic bag will exist on earth is **1,000 years.**
- Producing and recycling paper bags generates significantly more air and water pollution compared to plastic bags.
- **Paper is 40% of all waste.**
- The average family accumulates 60 plastic bags every 4 trips to the grocery store.
- San Francisco, the first city in the U.S. to ban the use of plastic grocery bags, eliminates the use of 100 million plastic bags a year.

TAKE ACTION TODAY

1. Buy several canvas shopping bags or use duffle bags that you already own.
Most trips to the store require more than one bag.
2. Purchase canvas bags made from recycled materials.
3. Keep your canvas bags in the trunk of your car—trips to the store are often spontaneous.
4. When purchasing only one or two items and you don't have a canvas bag, just carry the items out of the store **without a bag.**
5. If you forget your canvas bag, at least **avoid double-bagging.**

YOU MATTER

You would accumulate 1,000 fewer bags this year if you simply used a reusable bag when shopping, especially grocery shopping. Paper and plastic bags are an environmental killer—they biodegrade slowly or not at all, deplete energy and natural resources, endanger wildlife, and poison our soil and waterways. So, from now on, when a store clerk asks "Paper or plastic?" Proudly answer, "CANVAS."

Why wouldn't you?

Give a Hug

FACTS

- Stimulation by **touch is absolutely necessary** for physical and emotional well-being.
- **Touch is used to relieve pain**, depression, and anxiety; to enhance a child's development and IQ; and to nurture premature babies.
- Hugging **strengthens the immune system**, reduces stress, assists sleep, lowers blood pressure, and is an **antidote to depression.**
- Hugging bolsters a patient's will to live, dispels loneliness, eases fear, opens doors to buried feelings, builds self-esteem, fosters altruism, and **imparts feelings of belonging.**
- Hugging offers a wholesome alternative to promiscuity, alcohol, and drugs.
- People need **4 hugs a day for survival**, 8 for maintenance, and 12 for growth.

TAKE ACTION TODAY

1. Hug the people you care about today. Hug them in the morning, **hug them to say hello**, hug them because they bring you happiness, hug them to say good-bye, hug them to say **"I love you,"** hug them to show compassion, hug them if they are sad, hug them if they are hurting, hug them because they did something incredible, or **hug them just because.**
2. Hug a total stranger or someone you don't know all that well…but ask first.
3. Challenge yourself and your friends to keep track of how many hugs you gave or received today.
4. Notice how you feel at the end of your day of hugging.

YOU MATTER

If everyone hugged 4 people today—the minimum requirement for "survival"—that would add up to 1.2 billion hugs. **If everyone gave** 12 hugs—the number required for "growth"—the total would be 3.6 billion. So take the time to give 12 hugs today.

That hug might be exactly what those 12 people needed.

Listen, Play, Appreciate Music

- Over **70% of schools** are not able to maintain funding for the arts.
- Schools with music programs compared to schools without have **significantly higher graduation rates**, 90.2% compared to 72.9%, and **higher attendance rates**, 93.3% compared to 84.9%.
- Students with coursework in music appreciation score roughly **60 points higher** in verbal and **40 points higher** in math on the SAT than their non-arts peers.
- Early musical training increases brain development in language, reasoning, math, science, memory, creativity, expression, and spatial intelligence.
- Choral singers are nearly **twice as likely to be involved in charity work**— as both volunteers and donors—than the average person.
- Every human culture uses music to preserve and pass on its ideas and ideals.
- Music is not limited by age, gender, ethnicity, or time.

TAKE ACTION TODAY

1. **Listen** to your favorite music and sing, dance, clap, jam on your air guitar, and enjoy it like no one is watching.
2. Go see or buy tickets for a **live** music performance.
3. Sign up for music **lessons** for yourself or your family.
4. If you already sing or play an instrument, do it today or offer **to teach** someone who wants to learn.
5. **Donate** unused instruments to a local school, church, or music education center.
6. **Communicate** with your school-district administrators or national legislators. Write a letter of appreciation for the hard work they do and request continued funding for the arts.

YOU MATTER

Music is fun, expressive, imaginative, beautiful, energizing, relaxing, interesting, and freeing. Through music, we preserve our cultural heritage, celebrate our faith with praise and worship, remember events and experiences from the past, come together with friends and family, and express our emotions.

Music is the soundtrack of life.

Use Online Bill Pay
monday 44

FACTS

- On average, **4.8 pieces of mail are delivered every day to over 146 million addresses.**
- One of the fastest growing robbery crimes is identity theft by stealing mail.
- With password protection, more than one level of authentication, increased online security, and 100% protection in case of fraud, **online bill pay is much safer** than putting a check in the mailbox.
- **Internet use and electronic account monitoring is the fastest way to detect fraud and decrease losses from identity theft.**
- Banking information can be accessed via the Internet anytime, anywhere.
- **Paying bills online saves the average consumer $6 in stamps and 4 hours of time each month.**
- 18.5 million trees would be saved annually if consumers viewed and paid bills online.

TAKE ACTION TODAY

1. Go to your bank's Web site, click on "**Online Banking**," and follow the instructions to set up online bill pay.

2. Print out statements, view transactions, check balances, pay bills, transfer funds, and look for other financial information at your convenience.

3. Stop receiving bank statements and bills in the mail by signing up for online delivery.

4. If you're not able to connect online, then set up **automatic payments** over the phone. You may still receive a statement, but your payments will be automatically deducted from your bank account.

YOU MATTER

Online bill paying is more **cost-effective, more environmentally friendly, quicker, safer, and more convenient** than the traditional open-the-envelope, write-a-check, lick-the-stamp, and place-in-your-mailbox method.

Do you need any more compelling reasons?

A HOUSE
DOESN'T
ALWAYS
MEAN...
A HOME.

GET INVOLVED WITH FOSTER KIDS

FACTS

- **Over 500,000 children are in foster care and their average age is 10.**
- Approximately 46% of children are in nonrelative foster family homes, 24% are in relative foster homes, 18% are in group homes or institutions, 4% are in pre-adoptive homes, and 7% are in other placement types.
- 41% of the children are white, 32% are black, and 18% are Hispanic.
- **The average length of stay for all children currently in foster care is 2.4 years.**
- 14% of the children in foster care have been there for more than 5 years.
- **Over 51,000 children are adopted annually through the foster care system.**

TAKE ACTION TODAY

1. Find a foster care facility near you. **Contact them and ask how you can help.**
2. Sign up as a volunteer and get your family and friends involved.
3. Be prepared. Volunteers at a foster care facility can be involved in everything from outside physical activities to arts and crafts.
4. Become a foster parent or adopt a child.

YOU MATTER

Children in foster care have been abused, abandoned, and/or neglected. Many will not return to live with their parents or even a relative. **While we wish the statistics were different, it is up to us to provide the love and support these children need.** They didn't choose to be placed in foster care, **but we can choose to step into the gap and make a difference.** WHO TAUGHT YOU HOW TO RIDE A BIKE? SWIM? OR PREPARE FOR A MATH TEST? Whether you remember or not, those people cared...**and so can you.**

DON'T BE
CLOTHES-MINDED.

DONATE CLOTHES

monday
46

FACTS

- **20 billion pounds of clothing** and textiles are thrown away every year—an average of 68 pounds per person.
- **1.5 billion pairs of unworn** or barely worn shoes are lying in closets.
- Over **35 million people live in poverty** and have limited money to purchase new clothes.
- On average, 3 million men, women, and children are **homeless at some point each year.**
- 50% of all homeless women and children are **fleeing domestic violence**, usually with only the clothes on their backs.

CLOTHING DONATIONS TO QUALIFIED CHARITABLE ORGANIZATIONS ARE TAX DEDUCTIBLE.

YOU MATTER

Donating clothes is one of the **easiest ways** to affect someone's life in a very tangible and significant way. You can **help someone stay warm**, wear shoes without holes, dress properly for a job interview, or don a new outfit for school. Do you really need all those clothes filling up your closet? **Millions of other people do.**

TAKE ACTION TODAY

1. Contact a local shelter or organization that receives clothing donations and ask about any **specific clothing needs.**
2. Look through your closet for clothing, coats, shoes, suits, blankets, pillows, purses, briefcases, umbrellas, and scarves that are in **good condition** and that **you haven't used in a year or more.**
3. Organize **a clothing drive** at work, school, your place of worship, or in your neighborhood.
4. Wash or dry-clean items. Don't donate items that are stained or torn.
5. Fold and pack clothing in boxes, attach appropriate labels, then deliver them.
6. Consider giving directly to a homeless person.

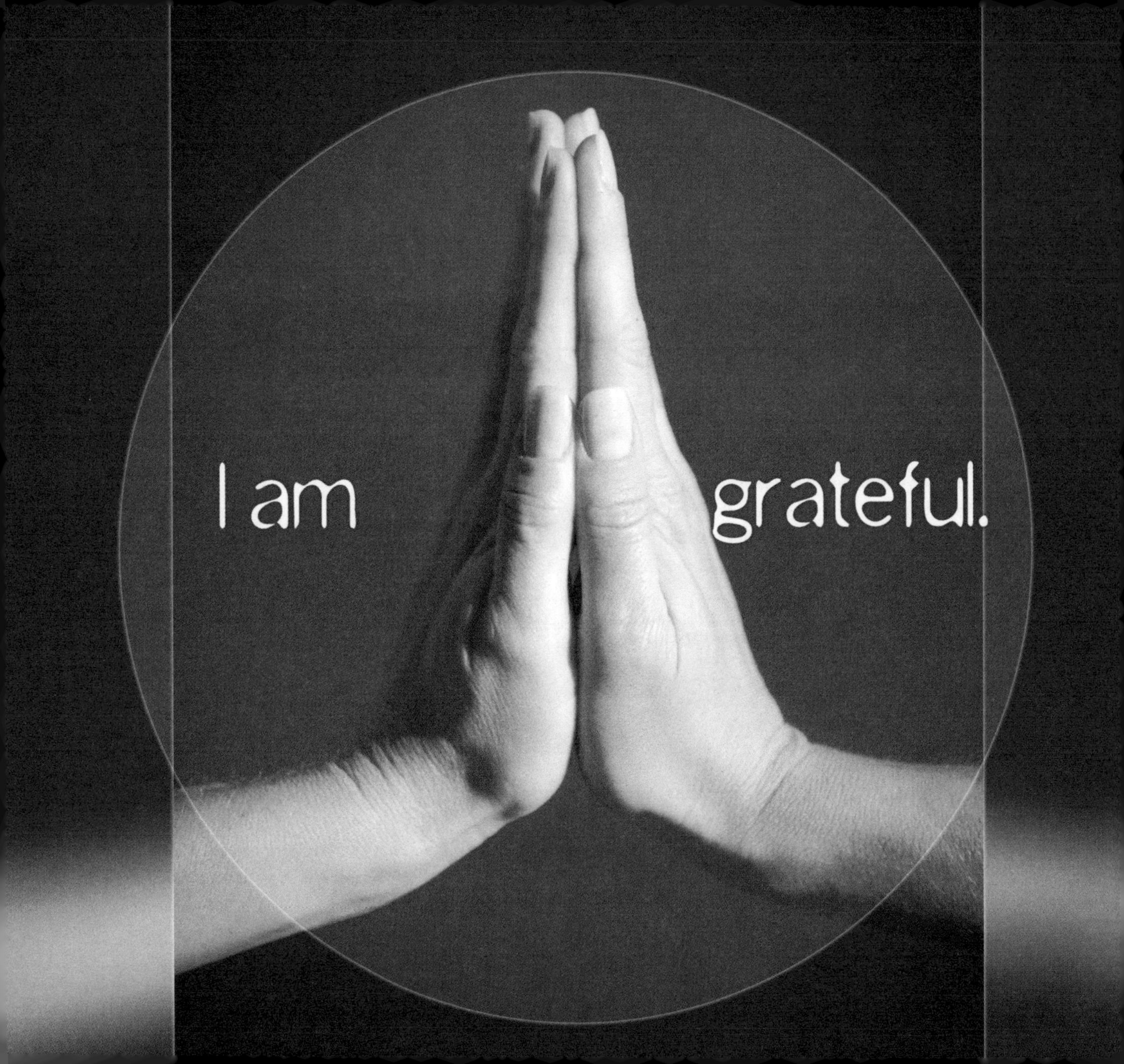
I am grateful.

Meditate or Pray

FACTS

- Meditation and prayer shift brain activity from the stress-prone right frontal cortex to the calmer left frontal cortex.
- Slowing the breathing rate to **6 breaths per minute** synchronizes breathing with cardiovascular rhythms resulting in enhanced cardiac health.
- Physiological benefits of prayer and meditation include **anti-aging,** deep rest, decreased blood pressure, higher skin resistance, and **easier breathing.**
- Psychological benefits include **increased brain-wave coherence**, greater creativity, decreased anxiety and depression, **improved learning and memory**, and increased **happiness and emotional stability.**
- The longer an individual practices meditation, the greater the likelihood that there will be a shift toward **personal and spiritual growth.**

TAKE ACTION TODAY

1. Find a quiet place to **be still.**
2. Take deep breaths to help you **relax.**
3. Meditate or pray.
4. With **a clearer mind**, journal your thoughts and insights.
5. Make meditation or prayer a part of your daily life.

YOU MATTER

Looking younger, lowered cholesterol and blood pressure, decreased anxiety and depression, *improved memory*, *increased happiness, more peace...*
what's not to like about meditating or praying?

RESERVED PARKING

RESPECT

Hillman Sign Center   Cincinnati, Ohio 45231   Made in U.S.A.   842168
03-0192-184

RESPECT THE DISABLED

FACTS

- **54 million** or more people ages 5 and older have a non-institutionalizing disability.
- **25 million disabled** are of an employable age.
- **78% want to be employed, but only 33% have a job.**
- Disabilities are more often caused by **accidents, illnesses, or late-emerging effects of genetics** than by congenital disorders.
- Not all severe disabilities can be detected by the human eye.
- **Over 15% of the cars parked in a handicapped parking space are parked illegally.**

TAKE ACTION TODAY

1. Show respect to the disabled today.
2. Don't park in a handicapped parking space or use handicapped plates or placards illegally.
Designated parking for the handicapped is a necessity.
3. Don't use handicapped bathroom stalls unless you're handicapped. A handicapped person's need to use the restroom may be just as urgent as yours, and it often takes them longer to prepare to use the facilities.
4. When you see a handicapped license plate, **slow down** and show consideration rather than tailgating or honking.
5. Open a door, roll a wheelchair up or down an incline, **carry shopping bags**, or offer an arm in challenging weather conditions or on uneven walkways.

YOU MATTER

The majority of people with disabilities want to be totally integrated into all aspects of society. **With more awareness, respect, and helpfulness, you can make someone's life a little bit easier.** *People don't plan on getting disabilities, but it happens every day.*

ONE DAY, THAT DISABLED PERSON MAY EVEN BE YOU.

you don't?

Reduce, Reuse, Recycle

FACTS

- The U.S. leads the industrialized world in waste generation, producing 245 million tons annually—4.5 pounds per person per day.
- **2.5 million** plastic bottles are thrown away every hour.
- **400 billion** photocopies are made every year—roughly **750,000 per minute.**
- Producing recycled white paper creates 74% less air pollutants, 35% less water pollutants, and 75% less process energy than producing paper from virgin fibers.
- Recycling an aluminum can saves **96% of the energy** used to make a can from ore and produces 95% less air pollution and 97% less water pollution.
- 32% of waste is recovered and recycled or composted, 14% is burned, and 54% is disposed of in landfills.
- **9,000 curbside recycling programs exist.**

Only 2 man-made structures on Earth are large enough to be seen from outer space—the Great Wall of China and the Fresh Kills Landfill in New York.

TAKE ACTION TODAY

1. **Reduce** what you use by purchasing larger sizes.
2. **Reuse rather than throw away.**
3. Contact your local waste management company and find out if they sort trash and recycle. If not, create different containers in your home and at work for **glass, plastic, and paper.**
4. Deliver your separated recyclables to a local **recycling center** once a month.
5. **Buy recycled products and packaging.**

YOU MATTER

Reducing, reusing, and recycling are key to protecting our resources and preserving our environment for future generations. Garbage means wasted water, wasted energy, pollution, transportation costs, and overflowing landfills. Reducing is the most powerful technique for eliminating waste because we don't generate waste in the first place. If reducing is out of the question, then at least reuse or recycle. You have three options.
WHICH ONE ARE YOU GOING TO CHOOSE TODAY?

It takes more than an apple.
I LOVE MY TEACHER! MY TEACHER IS GREAT!

Thank a Teacher

FACTS

- **There are 3.8 million teachers—2.6 million teach K-12.**
- **42% of K-12 teachers** are over 50 years old.
- Almost 50% of teachers leave the profession by their fifth year.
- **$7 billion** a year is the cost of teacher turnover.
- A $15 billion per year investment or a 30% raise for all teachers is necessary to make teacher compensation competitive with other professions requiring similar levels of education.
- **In 37 states, teacher salaries do not keep pace with inflation.**
- **The single most important factor in determining student performance is the quality of his or her teachers.**

TAKE ACTION TODAY

1. Identify a teacher you want to thank—your child's teacher, a friend or neighbor who teaches, a teacher at a local school, or a teacher of your own.
2. Show this teacher your appreciation by:
- **Writing** a thank-you note.
- **Bringing a gift** like homemade cookies, handpicked flowers, a book on a topic that interests them, or a gift card for something you know they will like.
- **Organizing** a class Appreciation Jar. Give every student a piece of paper and have them list all the reasons **why their teacher is special to them.** Stuff the papers in the jar and let the teacher open one per day.
- **Volunteering** in the classroom and helping with special projects or field trips.

YOU MATTER

Children are the future of our world, and teachers spend more waking hours with them than their parents do. Showing appreciation to teachers lets them know they are valued and respected—you don't have to be a student or even a parent of a student to **show your appreciation**.
Remember, teachers help shape everyone's world...including yours.

SURGEON GENERAL'S WARNING:
Cigarette Smoke
Contains Carbon Monoxide.

ADDICTED TO DYING?

NONICOTINE

FACTS

- Nicotine is as addictive as heroin or cocaine.
- **12 million deaths** have been caused by cigarette smoking over the last 40 years.
- **8.6 million** people have at least one serious illness caused by smoking.
- **80%** of adult smokers started smoking before the age of 18.
- **Every day 4,000 people under the age of 18 try their first cigarette, of which 80% become adult smokers.**
- Every year **$75 billion or more** is spent on cigarette-related medical conditions.
- **Nicotine can be found in the umbilical cord blood of a fetus during pregnancy as well as in breast milk.**
- 70% of smokers say they want to quit.
- 91.2% of all successful long-term quitters quit cold turkey, without the assistance of patches, gum, hypnosis, acupuncture, inhalers, or prescriptions.

TAKE ACTION TODAY

1. Stop smoking—do it cold turkey. Don't light up! And if you chew tobacco, avoid even a pinch today. **You can do it.**
2. Quit with a friend so that you can hold each other accountable.
3. If necessary, use one of the many nicotine replacement therapies.
4. If you are a nonsmoker, "adopt" a smoker. **Support them by giving encouragement**, exercising together, going out where there isn't likely to be smoking, and **providing comfort and accountability.**

YOU MATTER

There will be 1 billion fewer cigarettes smoked and 274 million fewer cigarette butts littered, if nobody lights up today. **People say it's hard to give up smoking, but isn't it harder to keep doing it?** To continue smoking, you have to pay for cigarettes, always have a light, get rid of the ashes, and figure out what to do with the butt. Oh...and **hope it doesn't kill you.**

MAY THIS ONE DAY OFF BE THE FIRST DAY OF THE REST OF YOUR OR YOUR FRIENDS' TOBACCO-FREE LIFE.

YES, WE ARE
POINTING AT YOU.

YOUR DAY

Today is your day.

Today you get to pick how you want to make a difference.

You know the drill. Think of something—and go do it.

PRETTY SIMPLE.

There is only one catch: we want to hear about it.

Let us know what you did and what resulted.

We will be selecting one of your ideas to be one of the "Mondays" in our next book.

So be creative, have fun, and make sure to let us know what you did to make today matter.

Go to **EVERYMONDAYMATTERS.COM**

to learn more about the "Your Day" Contest.

Thanks for taking this journey with us.

Every time you took care of yourself, did something for someone else,
protected the environment, gave from your heart, volunteered your time,
and donated your possessions, your action had a ripple effect on your friends, neighbors,
co-workers, community, city, country, and the world.

We are confident that you had an amazingly gratifying year
and that you know in your heart that you really did make a difference.
Every smile, every thank you, and every gesture of appreciation confirmed this for you.

YET THE WORK HAS JUST BEGUN.
IT'S A BIG WORLD OUT THERE.
NOW YOU UNDERSTAND JUST HOW MUCH YOU MATTER.

To the world you might be one PERSON,

but to one person you might BE THE WORLD.

- Unknown

Every Monday Matters
donates a portion of each book sale
to worthy charities around the world.

We have also launched the Every Monday Matters Foundation.
The goal of the foundation is to raise awareness
of organizations affecting change.
Please visit our list of charities at EveryMondayMatters.com.
Your donations matter.

Acknowledgments

You Mattered

Grandma Annie & Grandpa Charlie, Grandma Flo & Grandpa Art, Grandma & Poppo, Grandma Lola, Grandma McDonald.

You Matter

God, Mom & Dad Emerzian, Mom & Dr. Bozza, Eric, Melisa and Marlo Bozza, Michael, Melissa, Gavin and Kate Emerzian, and all of our families.

You Support the Soul

Temy Johnson, Raylene & Jim Creath, Bob Roeland, Denise McPhee, Tom & Laura Greanias, Elsa Bugarini, Jon Benak, Scott Turner, Gary Cooper, Alex Jones-Moreno, Kenton Beshore, Phillip & Holly Wagner, Keenan Barber, Kim, Bret, Brittany, Kristen, and Tanner Harrison, Felix Pfeifle, Andrew Paul Woodworth, Felice Gomez & family, Christine Rosasco, Kent Russell, Jody Hanford, Mark Todd, Keitha & Jim Haley, Kristy Kazmark, Cheri Ikerd, Christie Brockhage, Victoria Frensdorff, Frank Gordon, Judy Christensen, Darby Vajgrt, Rosio Paniagua, Juliann Powers, Tom Dobyns, Karen Norwood, Susan Burritt, Frank Greenfield, Patricia Bongo, Patrice Perrone, Shannon Sharp, Renny & Caren Temple, Nikki & Tony McIntosh, Leslie Murray, Leslie Minniti, Cindy Alexander, Chris Rong, Patrick Davern, The Alliance brothers, The Street Team, Sol Garcia, Amy Jokinen, Tami & Jeff Merry, Joe Clemens, Jamie Nations, Tarzan, Junior, Hagen, La Fogata, Banderas, Gallo Subs, Doughboys, Jones on 3rd, Toast, Swerve, Weho Pool, and the CdM tidepools.

You Helped

Our literary agent Erin Hosier; the Thomas Nelson family—Lisa Stilwell, Mark Gilroy, Troy Johnson, Jackie Johnston, MacKenzie Howard, Todd Shuttleworth, and Ariel Faulkner; Brian Neal, Brooke Ehrlich, Debbie Sheppard, Taj Tedrow, Ted Perez, Pier Tiano, Toni Lamb, Tony Orlando, Jon Orlando, David Brokaw, Aletta St. James, Rick Anderson, Tara Hanks, Carolyn Sams, Gene Howard, Martin Johnson, Michelle Walsh-Ozanne, Tanya Memme, Invisible Children, Nick Cannon, Benjamin McKenzie, Brooke Peterson, John Matoian, Dorian Graham, Emmy, The Oasis 3D Kids, Javier Prato, Richard Marks, Harold Brooks, Matt Brown.

A Very Special Thank You

Our partners Beau Gaynor, Richard Baker, William Fitzmaurice, Rebekah May, Matt Stoen, and the rest of the UTC Financial team.
Beau, your generosity has allowed us to reach more people through this book and the Every Monday Matters movement much sooner than we ever could have reached on our own.

Leonardo Canneto, Jay Dawg Brown, and Lisa Stilwell, your passion for your art brought these pages to life.

And for the many who helped us along the way and are not mentioned above, or we never knew your name in the first place, thank you for supporting the pursuit of dreams being realized and giving us so many reasons to matter.

Every Monday Matters
Research Sources

1. What Matters Most
Bond, James T. with Cindy Thompson, Ellen Galinsky, and David Prottas. Highlights of The National Study of the Changing Workforce Executive Summary. Families and Work Institute. No. 3, 2002.
Browning, Guy. "How to...waste time." The Weekend Guardian. March 4, 2006.
U.S. Department of Labor
U.S. Census Bureau

2. Turn Off Your TV
American Family Research Council
American Medical Association
Annenberg Public Policy Center
Barber, Benjamin. "America skips school: Why we talk so much about education and do so little." *Harper's*. November 1993: 41.
"Living Healthy, Working Well." State of California Employee Assistance Program Newsletter (distributed by Magellan of California). Vol. 7, No. 9. March 2001.
Nielsen Media Research
"Number of Sex Scenes on TV Nearly Double Since 1998." Kaiser Family Foundation. November 9, 2005.
Senate Judiciary Committee Staff Report. "Children, Violence, and the Media." 1999.
U.S. Department of Labor
Yankelovich MONITOR Perspective

3. Have AMBER Alerts Sent to You
Amberalert.gov. AMBER Alert: America's Missing Broadcast Emergency Response. U.S. Department of Justice
McKenna, Rob, Attorney General of Washington & U.S. Department of Justice Office of Juvenile Justice and Delinquency Prevention, with Katherine M. Brown, Robert D. Keppel, Joseph G. Weis, & Marvin E. Skeen. CASE MANAGEMENT for Missing Children Homicide Investigation. May 2006.
wirelessamberalerts.org: The Wireless Foundation

4. Prepare for an Emergency
Danville Police Department
Federal Emergency Management Agency
National Climatic Data Center in cooperation with the National Hurricane Center
National Geographic
National Oceanic and Atmospheric Administration National Weather Service
Ready America
Reuters Foundation
U.S. Department of Commerce
U.S. Department of Homeland Security

5. Eat Healthy
Centers for Disease Control and Prevention
Field, A. E., S. B. Austin, M. W. Gillman, B. Rosner, H. R. Rockett, and G. A. Colditz. "Snack food intake does not predict weight change among children and adolescents." *International Journal of Obesity* (2004) 28, 1210–1216. doi:10.1038/sj.ijo.0802762. Published online August 17, 2004.
Mokdad, Ali H., PhD, James S. Marks, MD, Donna F. Stroup, MPH, Julie L. Gerberding, MD, MPH. "Actual Causes of Death in the United States, 2000." JAMA, *the Journal of the American Medical Association*, 2004, vol. 291, n. 10, pp. 1238–1245.
National Institute of Mental Health
U.S. Department of Agriculture
Wolf A. M. and G. A. Colditz. "Current estimates of the economic cost of obesity in the United States." *Obesity Research* 6:97–106, 1998.

6. Get Rid of Junk Mail
Center for a New American Dream
Conservatree
Consumer Research
Department of Environment and Planning, Erie County
Postal Rate Commission
U.S. Department of Energy
U.S. Forest Service
Usjunkmail.com

7. Write a Letter to a U.S. Military Hero
Anysoldier.com
U.S. Department of Defense

8. Help the Hungry
America's Second Harvest–The Nation's Food Bank Network
Cromwell, Sharon. "Students Learn While Helping at Soup Kitchen."
Education World. 1999.
U.S. Census Bureau
U.S. Department of Agriculture

9. Protect Yourself with Internet Safety
Anti-Phishing Working Group
Better Business Bureau
FDIC
Javelin Strategy and Research
U.S. Census Bureau
Webopedia Computer Dictionary

10. Change Your Lightbulbs
Climatecrisis.net
U.S. Department of Energy
U.S. Environmental Protection Agency

11. Register to Vote
Andolina, Molly. The Civic and Political Health of the Nation. 2002.
Rusbasan, Bob. "Should People Bother to Vote?" March 2, 1999.
rubasan.com.
The Center for Information & Research on Civic Learning & Engagement
U.S. Census Bureau

12 . Party with a Purpose
Births, Marriages, Divorces, and Deaths: Provisional Data for 2005.
National Vital Statistics Reports. Vol. 54, No. 20. July 21, 2006.
First Data Corp. Press Release
Hallmark, updated June 2007.
Myvesta
U.S. Census Bureau

13. Donate Books
Dickinson, David K. and Susan B. Neuman. Handbook of Early Literacy
Research, Volume 2 (Guilford Press: New York, 2006).
Harris Interactive Inc.
McQuillan, Jeff. "The Literacy Crisis: False Claims, Real Solutions."
1998.
National Center for Family Literacy
The State of Literacy in America, 1998
U.S. Census Bureau
U.S. Department of Agriculture

14. Create, Support, Appreciate Art
Ad Council
Americans for the Arts
Harris Interactive Inc.
National Education Association Press Release
The College Board SAT, 2006. 2006 College-Bound Seniors: Total
Group Profile Report.

15. Rideshare
AAA
Alternative Fuels Data Center
American Community Survey
Colorado Pollution Prevention
National Safety Council
U.S. Department of Energy

16. Support Neighborhood Watch
Are We Safe? The National Crime Prevention Council with support from
ADT Security Services, Inc. 2000/2001 survey.
U.S. Department of Justice

17. Register to Donate Your Organs
Harris Interactive Inc.
Organ Procurement and Transplantation Network
U.S. Department of Health and Human Services
U.S. Government Information on Organ and Tissue Donation and Transplantation

18. Show Your Smile
Berk, L. S., S. A. Tan, W. F. Fry, B. J. Napier, J. W. Lee, R. W. Hubbard,
J. E. Lewis, and W. C. Eby (1989) "Neuroendrocrine and stress
hormone changes during mirthful laughter." American Journal of the
Medical Sciences, 298(6), 390–396.
Crystal, Gael, MD and Patrick Flanagan, MD. Laughter—Still the Best
Medicine.
Holden, Robert. Laughter—The Best Medicine. London, England:
Thorsons, 1995.
LaFrance, M., and M. A. Hecht (2000). "Why do women smile more than
men?" In A. Fischer (Ed.), Gender and emotions. (pp.118–142).
Cambridge: Cambridge University Press.
Milwaukee Journal Sentinel, February 24, 1997.
raisingkids.co.uk
Siegel, Bernie, MD. Peace, Love & Healing—Bodymind Communication
& the Path to Self-Healing: An Exploration. (Harper & Row: New York,
1989).
Thompson, J. "Development of facial expression of emotion in blind and
seeing children." Archives of Psychology in New York, 261, 1–47, 1941.

Every Monday Matters
Research Sources

19. Adopt a Pet
American Pet Products Manufacturers Association (APPMA) 2005/2006 National Pet Owners Survey.
Humane Society of the United States

20. Don't Flick Your Cigarette Butt
National Fire Protection Association
National Survey on Drug Use and Health
Ocean Conservancy International Coastal Cleanup
Register, Kathleen M. "Underwater Naturalist," *Bulletin of the American Littoral Society*, Volume 25, Number 2, August 2000.
U.S. Department of Agriculture

21. Learn CPR
American Heart Association

22. Thank a Firefighter
National Fire Protection Association
The Geneva Association World Fire Statistics
U.S. Fire Administration.

23. Get Tested
Alan Guttmacher Institute
American Social Health Association
Cates, J. R., N. L. Herndon, S. L. Schulz, J. E. Darroch (2004). *Our voices, our lives, our futures: Youth and sexually transmitted diseases.* Chapel Hill, NC: University of North Carolina at Chapel Hill School of Journalism and Mass Communication.
Chesson, H. W., J. M. Blandford, T. L. Gift, G. Tao, and K. L. Irwin. The estimated direct medical cost of STDs among American youth, 2000. Abstract P075. 2004 National STD Prevention Conference. Philadelphia, PA. March 8–11, 2004.
Koutsky L. (1997). "Epidemiology of genital human papillomavirus infection," *American Journal of Medicine*, 102(5A), 3–8.
National HIV Prevention Conference
U.S. Department of Health and Human Services
Weinstock, H., S. Berman, W. Cates. "Sexually transmitted diseases among American youth: incidence and prevalence estimates, 2000." *Perspectives on Sexual and Reproductive Health* 2004;36(1):6–10.

24. Don't Honk
California Vehicle Code
Noise Center at the League for the Hard of Hearing
Noise Pollution Clearinghouse

25. Plant a Tree
American Forestry Association
American Forests Press Release
Prow, Tina. "The Power of Trees," Human Environmental Research Laboratory at University of Illinois.
The Maryland Department of Natural Resources Forest Service
USDA Forest Service

26. Support a Global Cause
Children's Hunger Relief Fund
Food and Agriculture Organization
Global Poverty Monitoring, World Bank
Oxfam
UNICEF
United Nations High Commissioner for Refugees
United Nations World Food Program
World Health Organization

27. Protect Yourself from Identity Theft
Better Business Bureau
Javelin Strategy and Research

28. No Fast Food
Bowman, S. A, S. L. Gortmaker, C. B. Ebbeling, M. A. Pereira, D. S. Ludwig. "Effects of fast-food consumption on energy intake and diet quality among children in a national household survey," *Pediatrics.* 2004; 113: 112–118.
Fast Food and Quickservice Restaurants. First Research, Inc. May 21, 2007.
Nestle, M. *Food Politics: How the Food Industry Influences Nutrition and Health.* Berkeley, CA: University of California Press, 2002.
The 2003 California High School Fast Food Survey
U.S. Department of Health and Human Services
Young, L. R., and M. Nestle. "The contribution of expanding portion sizes to the U.S. obesity epidemic," *American Journal of Public Health.* 2002; 92:246–249.

29. Write a Note of Gratitude
CTIA-The Wireless Association
Department of Environment and Planning, Erie County.
Laschinger, Bernice, and Kate White. "Appreciation," *British Journal of Psychotherapy* Vol. 18 Issue 1, 106–109. September 2001.
Radicati Group, 2006

30. Create a Back-to-School Backpack
Center for Effective Parenting
kidsource.com
National Center for Children in Poverty
United Way, Alberta, Canada

31. Treat the Homeless with Dignity
Kroloff, Rabbi Charles A. "54 Ways You Can Help the Homeless."
National Coalition for the Homeless
National Law Center on Homelessness and Poverty
U.S. Conference of Mayors
U.S. Department of Housing and Urban Development
Urban Institute
Zorza, J. "Woman Battering: A Major Cause of Homelessness,"
Clearinghouse Review, 25(4) (1991). Qtd. In National Coalition Against
Domestic Violence, "The Importance of Financial Literacy, " October
2001.

32. Don't Drive over the Speed Limit
Insurance Institute for Highway Safety
National Highway Traffic Safety Administration
U.S. Department of Transportation

33. Read a Book
National Endowment for the Arts
U.S. Census Bureau

34. Pick Up Litter
Beverage Industry Environment Council, Sydney, Australia
Ocean Conservancy International Coastal Cleanup
U.S. Environmental Protection Agency

35. Go Exercise
He, J., P. K. Whelton. "Elevated systolic blood pressure and risk of car-
diovascular and renal disease: overview of evidence from observational
epidemiologic studies and randomized controlled trials," *American Heart
Journal* 1999 Sept; 138(3 Pt 2):211–219.
National Institute of Mental Health
Ogden, C. L., M. D. Carroll, L. R. Curtin, M. A. McDowell, C. J. Tabak, K.
M. Flegal. "Prevalence of overweight and obesity in the United States,
1999-2004," *JAMA, the Journal of the American Medical Association*,
295:1549–1555. 2006.
Robins, L. N., D. A. Regier (Eds). *Psychiatric Disorders in America, The
Epidemiologic Catchment Area Study*, 1990; New York: The Free Press.
U. S. Department of Health and Human Services

36. Be Neighborly
ApRoberts, Alison and Gina Kim. "A Sense of Community." The
Sacramento Bee. May 21, 2006.
American Community Survey
Families and Work Institute
Feldstein, Lewis and Robert Putnam. *Better Together: Restoring the
American Community* (Simon & Schuster: New York, 2003).
Marples, Gareth. "History of Garage Doors."
U.S. Bureau of Labor Statistics
U.S. Census Bureau

37. Mentor a Child
2006 National Agenda for Action: How to Close America's Mentoring
Gap, Mentor.
Big Brothers Big Sisters in conjunction with Public/Private Ventures
Burton, Paul E. *One-Third of a Nation: Rising Dropout Rates and
Declining Opportunities*. Policy Information Center, Educational Testing
Service, February 2005.
Green, Jay P., PhD, and Marcus A. Winters. Public High School
Graduation and College-Readiness Rates: 1991-2002. New York:
Manhattan Institute for Policy Research. No. 8. February 2005.
Mentoring as a Family Strengthening Strategy: Brief No. 4. Annie E.
Casey Foundation; National Human Services Assembly, 2004.
National Household Survey on Drug Abuse/Substance Abuse and
Mental Health Services Administration
No Child Left Behind
Swanson, Christoper B. "Who Graduates? Who Doesn't?: A Statistical
Portrait of Public High School Graduation, Class of 2001," Washington,
D. C.: The Urban Institute. February 2004.
The Silent Epidemic: Perspectives of High School Dropouts. John M.
Bridgeland, John J. Dilulio Jr., and Karen Burke Morison. A report by
Civic Enterprises in association with Peter D. Hart Research Associates
for the Bill & Melinda Gates Foundation, March 2006.

38. Donate Blood
American Association of Blood Banks
American Red Cross
America's Blood Centers
Chambers, Linda, MD, senior medical officer, Biomedical Services,
August 2001 and Sharron Siliva, director, Market Research, October
2001.
National Blood Data Resource Center
U. S. Department of Health and Human Services Advisory Committee
on Blood Safety and Availability

Every Monday Matters
Research Sources

39. Have Fun with an Elderly Person
National Center for Health Statistics, Centers for Disease Control and Prevention
National Institute on Aging
U.S. Census Bureau

40. Thank a Local Law Enforcement Officer
Federal Bureau of Investigation
U.S. Department of Justice

41. Choose Canvas Bags
American Forest Paper Association
Clean Up Australia
Film and Bag Federation, Society of the Plastics Industry
"San Francisco bans traditional plastic grocery bags," CBC News, March 28, 2007.
U.S. Environmental Protection Agency
Wall Street Journal

42. Give a Hug
Buscaglia, Leo, PhD
DeMarco, Donald. "Our Destiny to Live and Love," The Interim. January 2004.
Keating, Kathleen. *The Hug Therapy Book.* CompCare Publishers. 1983.
Ornish, Dean, MD. *Love and Survival: The Scientific Basis for the Healing Power of Intimacy.* Collins. 1999.

43. Listen, Play, Appreciate Music
Americans for the Arts
Chorus Impact Study, chorusamerica.org
College-Bound Seniors National Report: Profile of SAT Program Test Takers. Princeton, NJ: The College Entrance Examination Board, 2001. Harris Interactive Inc.
National Association for Music Education
National Education Association

44. Use Online Bill Pay
Better Business Bureau
Idealbite.com
Javelin Strategy and Research
Komando, Kim
LifeLock
National Crime Prevention Council
U. S. Postal Service

45. Get Involved with Foster Kids
U.S. Department of Health and Human Services

46. Donate Clothes
Internal Revenue Service
National Coalition for the Homeless
National Law Center on Homelessness and Poverty
Secondary Materials and Recycled Textiles Association
soles4souls.com
Urban Institute
U.S. Census Bureau

47. Meditate or Pray
Bernardi, L., P. Sleight, G. Bandinelli, S. Cencetti, L. Fattorini, J. Wdowczyc-Szulc, A. Lagi. "Effect of rosary prayer and yoga mantras on autonomic cardiovascular rhythms: comparative study," *British Medical Journal.* 2001;323:1446-9.
Davidson, Richard J., Jon Kabat-Zinn, Jessica Schumacher, Melissa Rosenkranz, Daniel Muller, Saki F. Santorelli, Ferris Urbanowski, Anne Harrington, Katherine Bonus, and John F. Sheridan. "Alterations in Brain and Immune Function Produced by Mindfulness Meditation," *Psychosomatic Medicine.* 65: 564–570, 2003.
National Center for Complementary and Alternative Medicine, National Institutes of Health.

48. Respect the Disabled
American Association of People with Disabilities
Taylor, C. J. (1998). "Factors affecting behavior towards people with disabilities," *Journal of Social Psychology,* 138(6), p. 766–771.
U.S. Census Bureau
U.S. Department of Health and Human Services
Wikipedia, The Free Encyclopedia.

49. Reduce, Reuse, Recycle
Clean Air Council
U.S. Environmental Protection Agency

50. Thank a Teacher
Alliance for Excellent Education
American Federation of Teachers
Hernandez, Nelson. "Teacher Turnover Costs Systems Millions, Study
Projects." Washingtonpost.com, Thursday, June 21, 2007.
National Center for Education Information
National Center for Education Statistics
National Education Association
U.S. Bureau of Labor Statistics

51. No Nicotine
American Cancer Society
Center for Health Promotion and Education
Centers for Disease Control and Prevention
Office on Smoking and Health
U.S. Department of Health and Human Services

Check out our CD-ROM providing exclusive links
to access special portions of our Web site.

Watch how other people are making a difference,
as well as get ideas for shooting your own
Every Monday Matters videos.